The Business Idea

Søren Hougaard

The Business Idea

The Early Stages of Entrepreneurship

With 20 Figures and 17 Tables

 Springer

Søren Hougaard
3 Loevvaenget
2960 Rungsted Kyst
Denmark
shougaard@amsgroup.dk

Co-publication by Springer Heidelberg, Germany
and Samfundslitteratur, Frederiksberg, Denmark.
The original was published in 2004, ISBN 87-593-1106-1
The Danish title is: Forretningsidéen

Cataloging-in-Publication Data
Library of Congress Control Number: 2004112219

ISBN 3-540-22663-X Springer Berlin Heidelberg New York

Springer is a part of Springer Science+Business Media

springeronline.com

© Springer Berlin · Heidelberg 2005
Printed in Germany

Hardcover-Design: Erich Kirchner, Heidelberg

SPIN 11307839   42/3130-5 4 3 2 1 0 – Printed on acid-free paper

Contents

Preface

The expectation that a society in which there is a high level of innovation and entrepreneurship will be more robust and provide better opportunities for growth has put entrepreneurship at the top of the political agenda of the western world.

The established business community is, in fact, the primary source of new venture activities, which is why the presence in the economy of innovative and expansive businesses is advantageous for entrepreneurship rather than the opposite. However, if intra- and entrepreneurship is to provide momentum, this engine – like all other engines – needs fuel and conditions contributing to opportunities and competencies.

The work behind the present book is based both on theory and practice, more specifically on my personal experience from an everyday life full of start-up projects, product development, strategic marketing dilemmas, business plans, risk assessment and decisions taken under uncertainty. These are often tough nuts to crack in a situation where the likelihood of being wrong is ever present and where failure is costly.

During my many years as an entrepreneur and innovator, I have become acquainted with lots of ideas, strategies and plans. It has always been a puzzle to me why there is so much focus on *business plans*, but so little on *business ideas*. A good friend was asked recently whether he would be interested in investing in a start-up project. His conclusion afterwards was the following: "These young people have prepared an amazing business plan; the trouble is that there is no business idea behind it!" Exactly this state of affairs is characteristic of a lot of entrepreneurial undertakings.

One reason for this apparent lack of attention and focus on the business idea is probably an annoying deficit of methodology and techniques What do you do to develop a competitive business idea, and how can you tell whether it is sustainable?

From the wide range of factors that determine whether a business idea will be successful or not, I have chosen to concentrate on a single dimension, i.e. *the market*, in the sense of customers and competitors. Not because there is anything surprising about the fact that market forces play a crucial role in determining whether or not a business idea will be successful, but rather because the cross-field between entrepreneurship and market is in desperate need of major methodological enhancement.

As my academic work is strategic marketing, and as all successful strategic marketing efforts will always contain elements of excellent entrepreneurship, it seemed natural to seek to combine the conceptual framework of marketing economics and the start-up situation, symbolised by the question: How can models, lines of thought and methods that are all well-known in marketing be translated into concrete, serviceable techniques for entrepreneurship?

The result of my work is the present book, *The Business Idea – the early stages of entrepreneurship.*

I owe a debt of gratitude to a number of people for their contribution to the process. This goes for my academic sparring partners, who have read and commented on my manuscript – some of them several times. My colleagues Associate Professors Henrik Johansen Duus and Kenneth Husted, both at Copenhagen Business School, have applied their very professional skills to the systematics, conceptual framework and use of literature in the book. My business friend Lars Ole Kornum, Managing Director, has read the manuscript closely and been very helpful in improving the instructive value of the text while confronting me with a number of relevant, practical questions. My son, Lars Hougaard, MSc Econ, MIF, has, in his usual mature and analytical manner, pointed to a considerable number of areas in which there was room for improvement in the project – almost all of which have been incorporated in the final manuscript.

Lena Fluger has been an exemplary editorial and language anchor, and to her, too, I am indebted.

This book contains many examples from real-life projects, some of which have been tremendous successes while others have had to be given up. I have tried to report these cases loyally and without compromising anybody involved; I know from experience that the risk of failure and loss is an inseparable part of being an entrepreneur.

In the years to come, I plan to gather additional material on the early stages of entrepreneurship in order to be able to contribute further knowledge and systematics that may be used in those crucial moments when the foundations for future business are laid.

Rungsted Kyst, Denmark
July 2004
Søren Hougaard

Introduction and summary

Vision

The vision of *The Business Idea* is to present and explain the entrepreneurial process from the moment an idea is conceived until the new business or business unit is introduced on the market. *The Business Idea* is a framework intended to sharpen your senses towards entrepreneurship and perhaps make you want to have a go at it yourself. The book aims at being both educational and a source of inspiration. The focus of *The Business Idea* is the concrete business venture – not the societal perspective.

In order to follow the book's vision with sufficient energy and directness, I have chosen one specific approach to the issue of entrepreneurship, which implies that other aspects, perhaps just as intriguing, have been left out. The approach I have chosen may be defined as follows:

Firstly, the book deals with the early stages of establishing an enterprise or business activity – the initial meeting between business idea and market: opportunity, concept, barriers and entry. In the book, I call this the showdown. Excellent entrepreneurship does not stop at the first, immediate market acceptance: that is where it all begins. The market decides whether the business venture can continue or perishes – whether it survived the showdown. This is why this phase is all-important.

Secondly, the starting point of *The Business Idea* is uncompromisingly market-orientated. It is often much harder to discover a problem and understand what makes it a problem – and thus the germ of an opportunity – than it is to develop solutions. This point of view should not be seen as if I am underestimating the importance of technological breakthroughs or the ability to create excellent products. It is a fact, however, that many business ventures stumble in their misguided search for a position of strength that relies on an uncritical belief in technology, product superiority and physical attributes, while their

9

customers struggle with problems and needs that are completely unrelated to technological advances or paradigm shifts, which makes them reluctant to embrace new inventions – and this in turn often leads to painful experiences for the entrepreneur.

And *thirdly*, the book presents provokingly general thoughts on the edges and potential of entrepreneurial ventures that are somewhat contrary to received wisdom. For example, *The Business Idea* claims that fierce competition is better than no competition, and that first mover advantages are often exaggerated or imaginary.

The book is based on market conditions, and its frame of reference consists of principles, methods and processes that may be used to combine special competencies with market insight to create a business opportunity. At no point does this narrow optic underestimate the factors of surprise or talent.

Composition

The Business Idea makes use of various kinds of sources interwoven in a close pattern which should, hopefully, come across as a well-balanced, logical entity. Its purpose is not to deduce and generalise on an abstract basis only; nor is it the intention to draw conclusions from one single case and generalise for all other cases. This book has been composed by lending, condensing, relating, combining, translating and exemplifying existing material. Its original contribution lies in its flow and focus – its composition – rather than in independent contributions to the existing knowledge about entrepreneurship.[1]

Four threads are interwoven:

- Theories on entrepreneurship, market-related strategy and competitive advantage at business level. In this respect you will be hard pushed to find

---

1   *The Business Idea* contains an interaction between life inside the individual business venture and a cool distance to it. Thus, conclusions and generalisations have been created in a combined interaction between people and projects going through the entrepreneurial phase, and an interpretation of such situations. This process must necessarily be characterised by alternating enthusiasm, empathy and antipathy in order to be interpreted and put into perspective.

better ideas than those of classics such as Abell, Drucker, Porter, Prahalad & Hamel, Day, Levitt, D'Aveni, if you are interested in the individual business venture.

- Typologies and models that are partly deduced from formal theories and partly consist of necessary, practical concepts. The models deal with central topics related to market-orientated entrepreneurship and may be used as guidelines in specific situations. In this way they become integral elements of the frame of reference.

- Examples and cases support and illustrate formal theories and increase the legitimacy of the outline. In addition, the examples may function as independent inspirational cases and as points of confrontation for the individual who is working on an entrepreneurial problem in practice or in the course of a study programme.

- Personal experience and events. It is debatable whether this aspect has any predictive value. On the other hand the qualitative generalisation – the case method – may be said to be quite reliable, if sources are sufficiently varied and the observer sufficiently unbiased. Whatever the case may be, many years of intimate association with entrepreneurship have shown that people of experience – good and less good – have a lot of relevant messages to send. Entrepreneurship bears many similarities to craftsmanship.

The vision is to formulate, illustrate and communicate information on the progression of the various stages of entrepreneurship and in so doing to present a conceptual framework for the meeting between the new business idea and the market. This is done through an interchange between theory and practice and between presentation, discussion and generalisation.

Progression

The choreography of *The Business Idea* is the driving force of markets opposite the ingenuity of the entrepreneur. The progression of the book – its ongoing logic – reflects the development that begins with the entrepreneur's very special motives, ideas and competencies and ends with the hopefully successful introduction of the new business venture on the market. The progression that the reader may expect is the unfolding of the entrepreneurial process into a sort of simulation or mental trip that goes from the individual's deliberation over goals and motives to the introduction of the young business on the market:

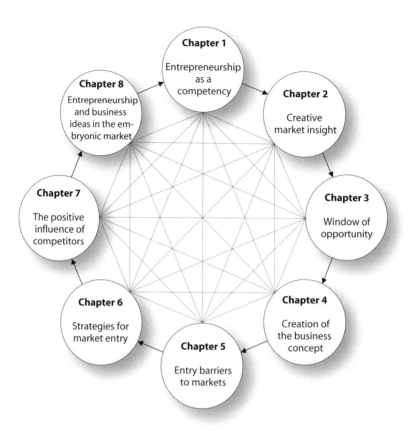

Fig. 0.1: The Business Idea – progression

The sequential design of business ventures into a few – limited – stages is the guiding principle of *The Business Idea*. The book offers a sequential model for entrepreneurship in a market perspective as shown in the figure, but does not provide a list of correct answers. Do not expect a manual of quick recipes for instant sales success. The book is full of theories, of unsuccessful business ventures and of doubt. But its undertone is basically positive: *Get cracking – a lot more people could become capable entrepreneurs.*

Scope of application

The purpose of *The Business Idea* is both narrow and broad. The *narrow purpose* lies in its foundations and approach expressed in the question:

How is it possible to *create* business opportunities by creatively *understanding* a market and by *combining* this understanding with the competencies encompassed by the individual business venture?

This approach to innovation and entrepreneurship is a major element in marketing as a discipline, and it narrows down the natural applications of this book in relation to the aggregate relevant subject and functional areas that are, in practice, also vital elements of successful entrepreneurship; this includes financing, project management, preparation of business plans, technology assessment, organisational development, general management, decision theory in risk situations etc.

The subject of the book is the market and the extent to which viable – often unexpected – business ideas may be born from empathy, insight, creativity and knowledge. The scope of the book is thus restricted to systematics and methods for developing innovative business ideas – which should not be confused with fantastic products.

The *broader objective* of the book is that the philosophy and models for business creation that is provided should make a positive contribution in many different contexts. Any person who works with, wants to know more about, or is studying the subjects of innovation and entrepreneurship may find *The Business Idea* useful. The book is suitable for teaching purposes as well as for practical use in start-up situations or in connection with consultancy and development guidance. *The Business Idea* may be used at a very concrete level for methodological support, skills enhancement or as a source of inspiration and motivation.

Summary

Chapter 1, Entrepreneurship as a competency, lays the foundations. This chapter defines the concept of entrepreneurship and helps the reader evaluate his or her own competency profile in an imaginary entrepreneurial role. Business ventures are propelled by people's sense of opportunity. Opportunities result from creation, the ability to see and understand problems and develop unexpected solutions. The conclusion is that entrepreneurship is not a privilege belonging to a small, select group of special personalities, but that it can be regarded as a social construction arising anywhere and involving anybody.

Entrepreneurship is teamwork, and Chapter 1 presents the basic competencies of entrepreneurship: the analytical-diagnostic force, the creative-innovative force and the interactive-communicative force. Successful ventures encompass and unite these *Graces*, preventing an imbalance from occurring.

The chapter also outlines the concepts of *invention* – technical perfection without any immediate commercial value – as opposed to *innovation*, which is the development of new methods, processes and products – i.e. applications widely compared to *entrepreneurship*, at the core of which are the opportunity and the chance to do something differently, better or at lower cost.

The basic thesis of *The Business Idea* is that it is possible to learn entrepreneurship, and that sustainable ideas require equal, dynamic interaction between very disparate competencies and thus between people.

Chapter 2 focuses on *creative market insight*. The innovative quality of strong business ideas is the unexpected solution. The unexpected solution is often founded on creative market insight – which should not be confused with conventional market insight. To uncover the unknown, to be able to look at the market and at needs from new angles requires profound knowledge and special skills. The chapter evolves around *the Four-Leaf-Clover Model*, i.e. four main roads leading to unique understanding of problems and opportunities. These are:

a) Occurrences i.e. events and changes – both unrecognised and well-known – that open the door to new business ventures created through the entrepreneur's interpretation and combination of information to develop opportunities;

b) Incongruities – latent weaknesses – that are just waiting to be discovered and remedied;

c) Innovation that creates needs and makes opportunities stand out. Innovation very often consists of technological achievements combined with new processes, materials or forms of organisation that add up to conditions for opportunity;

d) Missing links: obvious shortcomings, weak links, etc. that everyone has become used to, but which may be eliminated if you can catch sight of the blockages.

Even though Chapter 2 suggests that finding openings is about systematics and detailed knowledge, the element of surprise will always determine whether an opening holds potential financial value.

14

One possibility is, of course, the opportunity of meeting a market need by means of a creative combination of resources, which will lead to exceptional value. *Chapter 3* focuses on this *window of opportunity*. The perceptual window implies that the opportunity impulse is creative insight into the market, as distinct from the conceptual window; here the window of opportunity is created by the entrepreneur's special competencies. This distinction leads to four types of strategic windows: Problem solving, business formation, technology transfer and dream.

Chapter 3 also presents and describes the *grid of opportunity* – a method that allows the new venture to test its business idea in relation to the combination of customer lifecycle and field of value; in short, how and why an idea or a concept may create exceptional value. The grid of opportunity is the acid test for customer understanding and identification of needs.

The chapter then moves on to present the link between opportunity and congregation: many entrepreneurs have a preconceived idea that product superiority is a necessary and sufficient condition for success. As a consequence they risk underestimating the importance of reaching the very target group for whom innovation makes all the difference – as, for example, in the case of Nike and long-distance runners.

The chapter ends with a couple of tricky paradoxes, dogma killers, concerning the window of opportunity. Their special purpose is to make the entrepreneur take a critical stance on some of the factors that are usually regarded as the aces of a business venture. These factors include: the technical level of innovation, absence of competition, the number of interesting customer segments, the fact that major changes lead to great opportunities and that trusted friends are the most important source of inspiration.

From finding market openings and identifying the window of opportunity, *Chapter 4* takes a further step into the entrepreneurial process, i.e. to the *creation of the business concept*, symbolised by the question of how to define the business.

Reaching a sustainable business definition is a separate and challenging process. The business definition will often be the innovation itself. The business concept is created through the processing of and decision on three basic dimensions or axes, namely: customer groups (who), functions (by what means) and technologies (how). Business concepts may be divided into three main groups based on their level of focus and differentiation:

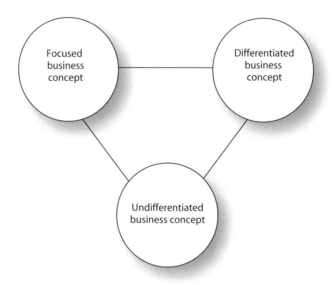

Figure 0.2 Business concepts

A *focused business concept* concentrates on one and only one of the three basic dimensions mentioned above, e.g. one particular customer group. A *differentiated business concept* seeks broad market appeal, differentiating by one or more of the dimensions in relation to customers or different needs. The *undifferentiated business concept* entails that the new enterprise defines its business broadly in relation to all three basic dimensions while, at the same time, refraining from differentiating the way in which the enterprise is organised vis-à-vis competitors or across customer segments.

There are many different factors that need to be incorporated when the new venture is defining its business concept, as a minimum the following: (1) buyer behaviour – differences in need and price sensitivity, (2) resource and competency requirements and (3) cost ratios – how pronounced and inevitable are the economies of experience and scale, and finally (4) the chance of redefining the market.

One good example of this is DDH, a Danish organisation that was founded in 1866 with the purpose of making the moors of Jutland arable. The organisation still exists even though its mission has long since been fulfilled. Why? The DDH did not define its business as agriculture but as landscape protection.

Visionary and sustainable business concepts have to relate to *market entry barriers*, which are the topic of *Chapter 5*. Entry barriers are obstacles and opponents

16

that affect the chances of new businesses and products of gaining a foothold in the market – the very first prerequisite for success. Chapter 5 operates with three categories of entry barriers:

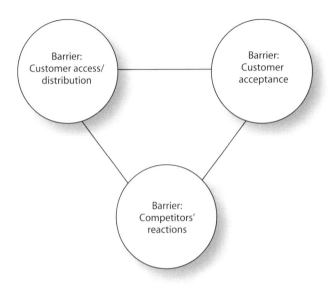

Fig. 0.3 Main categories of entry barriers

Only a fool does not fear obstacles to market entry. *Customer access* – distribution – is, in many cases, the most critical success factor, and requires special attention; distribution and positioning in the overall value chain must be incorporated into the business concept as well as into the business model chosen. This is evident within the IT/software sector where talented entrepreneurial projects tend to suffer an early death due to e.g. lack of customer access, caused by the fact that, from day one, unimpeded, efficient, transnational distribution is one of the business sector's most critical success factors. Capital requirements, fear of cannibalisation and retaliation from established suppliers are other factors that may reduce a new company's access to customers.

Customer acceptance presupposes that the new venture is able to match the cost and quality protection of established suppliers, symbolised by the perceived relative price and quality. Factors such as economies of scale, experience, systems ties, transaction costs, product differentiation, compatibility, references and brand value may individually or in combination amount to terrifying entry barriers for an upstart with few resources.

Competitor reaction is often – for very good reasons – deadly. The chapter contains an indicator system for expected competitor reaction: which information suggests swift and powerful versus weak and slow retaliation from established market players?

Chapter 5 also presents a number of less conventional ways for an entrepreneur venture to *overcome the entry barriers*. They have been structured under four headings: (1) the Trojan Horse – disguising to avoid otherwise impregnable defences, (2) Riding a Tiger – follow Microsoft's lead (!!!). (3) The Moving Target – using agility to prevent destruction, and (4) Jack the Dullard – a strategy based on counter-positioning and actually profiting from the investments made by others.

Chapter 5 ends with an inventory, the *barrier wheel,* in which the entrepreneur project may draw a profile of its specific, situational entry barriers.

The meeting of the new enterprise with the market is the moment of truth: Will we be accepted? Will customers hesitate? Will the business concept stand up? How will competitors react? *Chapter 6* contains detailed studies of *strategies for market entry.* The room for manoeuvre of the entry strategy is affected by the individual's unique competencies, but also to a considerable degree by market conditions: munificent or hostile, well-known or unknown.

The chapter outlines and discusses three different main roads to market introduction:

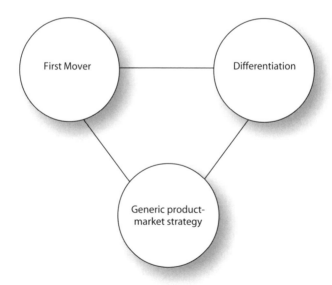

Fig. 0.4. Roads to market entry

The *first mover strategy* – first, biggest, best – is a classic and closely associated with some of the greatest stories in business history. During the dot.com bubble, the concept of first mover became a mantra. Some situations undoubtedly offer excellent opportunities of achieving pioneer advantages, such as experience based dominance, knowledge and loyalty, supplier relations, establishing business standards, not to mention monopolistic profits. However, the related risks pull in the opposite direction: market volatility, high pioneering costs, technological turbulence and so on.

As a successful first mover you need a clear vision for the mass market, managerial staying power, long-term financial power and relentless innovation. In practice, the notion that best beats first – not the other way around – is still valid.

Effective *differentiation* as an entry strategy may take several forms: strengthening the market's present sources of differentiation, reconfiguring the entire value chain, changing the rules and logic of business sectors or just cutting down differentiation costs, e.g. by exploiting cost-free differentiation benefits or by controlling crucial cost-generating elements.

Whereas differentiation in this context is based on the content of the new enterprise' unique offer, *generic product market strategies* deal with positioning in relation to the product and market spectrum that distinguishes between (1) a focus on niche, (2) a broad product range for a narrow market, (3) a narrow product range for a broad market, and (4) a modified niche that gives the new business the option of offering comparable products to closely related segments.

Competition is usually and justifiably seen as a threat to a newly started enterprise. That is why it might appear somewhat provocative when *Chapter 7* introduces *the positive influence of competitors*. In practice, however, competitors may be viewed, directly or indirectly, as facilitators of new business ventures, such as listed in the statements below:

1. Competitors create niches for others
2. Competitors pave the way for complementary products
3. Standards introduced by competitors act as midwives for new ventures
4. Competitors open the gate because customers want alternatives
5. Competition creates a basis for differentiation
6. Competitors stimulate the overall market

7. Competitors reduce customers' risks
8. Competitors reinforce success-creating industry factors for entrepreneurs
9. Competitors motivate entrepreneurs
10. A market-leading competitor holds up a cost umbrella.

Seen from the perspective of a newly started business, good market leaders are characterised by behaving nobly, albeit unconsciously, by giving high priority to short-term profitability, by enjoying moderate exit costs as well as loyal customers with high change-over costs. The opposite goes for harmful market leaders.

A slightly different angle on competitor types that create especially favourable conditions for entrepreneurs can be found in the caricatured distinction between: (a) The Good King, who shows magnanimity because he is convinced that he is invincible and reigns supreme, (b) The Wounded Giant, who is forced into short-term, tactical optimisation in order to defend himself against attacks from all sides, (c) The Cyclops, the one-eyed, cruel creature who defends his territory by all possible means, but who suffers from tunnel vision and fails to challenge himself, and (d) The Confident Tiger, fast and strong with no actual enemies.

Chapter 7 attempts to turn a problem that is often treated as an unambiguous threat into a positive, active element, i.e. a generator of opportunity, for those who know how to take a creative and opportunistic approach to the competitive environment

The concluding *Chapter 8* deals with quite a special and complicated issue: How is it possible to evaluate the conditions for *entrepreneurship in the embryonic market*? It is, after all, in the early life cycle stages of business sectors, markets and products that entrepreneurial activities are at their peak and entry barriers at their lowest.

Chapter 8 goes through various methods and approaches to understanding the impulses and forces that determine market births and life cycles. These methods are listed below.

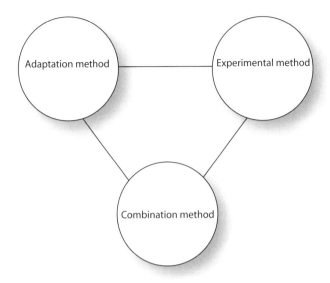

Fig. 0.5 Analysis of the embryonic market

The Adaptation Method focuses on the dissemination of innovation – the diffusion process. The diffusion of innovation depends on the strategic choices made by the players, the creation of effective standards, as well as stimulation of and acquisition in all major distribution channels. It is important to understand which and how strong an impact is required to disseminate innovation from a few enthusiasts over visionary adaptors to pragmatists – the mass market. Does this happen as a result of push and pull? Does the acquisition take place hierarchically, geographically and spatially, incorporated in products or …? What benefits, barriers and risks may be uncovered? What about reversibility and compatibility?

In actual fact it rarely ever happens that the net benefits of innovation are immediately and unconditionally superior to existing solutions, even though this is a fact that may be hard to swallow for those who want to get ahead.

Whereas the adaptation method includes scenarios and simulation, *the experimental method* deals with market learning by continuous trial and error. One of the most successful examples of market learning is Palm. Through customer reactions to successive, early – not particularly successful – launchings of Personal Digital Assistants, Palm realised that consumers regarded PDAs as small electronic diaries to replace their paper diaries rather than small, wireless computers, which was how their major competitors saw them. The discovery that Palm made through these tests led, among other things, to the special Palm graffiti system and elimination of the keyboard: simplification and minimisation.

The combination method means that you try to study the same central questions about the prospective market by using different sources, techniques and approaches to create a persistent strategy, but also the flexibility that arises out of conflict. Some of the sources that may be favourably combined include:

- Learning from potential clients that are at the cutting edge of the prospective market or analogous markets;
- Learning about latent needs – such as through problem identification, storytelling and observation;
- Prediction of turning points in lifecycles, determining factors and consequences.

At the end of the day, divergent thinking in an organisation, the motivation to explore new ways, the combination of the individual's desire to explore hypotheses and respect for the collective need for agreement all determine whether ideas become a reality.

As mentioned above, *The Business Idea* is not intended as a recipe for success – which should be obvious from some of the cases mentioned in the book – but rather as a tool to increase the chance of success within a field where most dreams remain just that – dreams.

1. Entrepreneurship as a competency

"The incentive of the entrepreneur is to try to get something for nothing, if only one can see what it is that can be done."

Israel M. Kirzner

When you have seen the birth of a great many business ideas, it becomes clear that there is no simple explanation of how they arise or why some are successful while others fail. The spectrum is wide and its diversity overwhelming. Just when you think you have uncovered logical patterns and sustainable correlations, some annoying inconsistencies will crop up.

The genesis of business ideas has to do with discovering and enabling. Behind enterprise we find individuals' sense of and faith in opportunities, irrespective of whether the origin of these perceptions is technical, production orientated or market based.

This introductory chapter focuses on the core of all ventures, i.e., the entrepreneur and his or her competency – the prerequisite for the business idea ever being conceived. The conclusion is that developing a robust business idea requires a wide range of competencies and energies that are only rarely present in one single individual. Entrepreneurship should be seen as a social construction and not as a biological phenomenon taking the form of rare personal qualities.

The chapter introduces the basic competencies of the entrepreneur, here termed the three Graces: analysis, creativity and communication. The chapter describes the two contrasting poles for the origin of business ideas – problem orientated versus solution focused entrepreneurship, just as the concepts of invention, innovation and entrepreneurship are related to the conception of the business idea.

The point of departure is that entrepreneurship can be learnt, that it consists of coherent processes and is executed in equal interaction between a number of different competencies.

1.1 Entrepreneurship as a concept

Winston Churchill is reputed to have said, "It is rather difficult to define an elephant, but you are not in doubt when you see one!" In a way, this is true of the excellent entrepreneurship – a concept surrounded by mystique and difficult boundaries.[2]

In *The Business Idea,* the centre of gravity is the individual business initiative, and with this purpose in mind, the broad societal definition of concepts is less central. A successful entrepreneur[3] has provided his own simple explanation of the concept, "It's really quite simple: use your common sense, listen to people, and seize opportunities as they arise". Getting something for nothing.

There is a lot of truth in this statement. First and foremost, it subscribes to a market rather than a product-orientated approach. It views identification and processing of the very opportunity as the primary competency of the entrepreneur. Its real foundation is that the ability to exploit opportunities presupposes an ability to see a problem and choose the right timing.

Peter F. Drucker (1986) leans in the same direction:

il "Because the problems which an entrepreneur faces are ill structured, entrepreneurship is not primarily about solving a problem, but rather about making an attempt to explain why it *is* a problem in the first place".

The problem orientated point of departure for entrepreneurship focuses on information, insight, empathy, and the narrowing down of needs and opportunities; it emphasises the art of surprise and, thus, the combination of creativity, knowledge, analysis and audacity.

The traditional statistical perception of the entrepreneur does not distinguish between the sole trader and the entrepreneur. That is to say an

---

2 In the literature, we find many varied definitions of entrepreneurship as a phenomenon depending on the level of scrutiny and professional platform of the observer. Definitions do not seem to constitute a pattern of progression of understanding. The word 'entrepreneur' is French and means an enterprising individual. Theories of why some individuals are more entrepreneurial than others: Personality theories (achievement, psychodynamics etc), behavioural theories, economic approaches, sociological approaches

3 Johnny Laursen, founder of the Danish publishing house Benjamin in 2003.

individual who organises and combines the factors of production with the purpose of making a profit. We might describe the entrepreneur as a *creator of equilibrium*, as this type of enterprise can be said to contribute to pushing the economic cycle towards equilibrium: optimal utilisation of resources and efficient price formation. The entrepreneur solves a problem, eliminates an incongruity in the economy, and so contributing to moving it towards equilibrium.

This explanation is not in accordance with a dynamic model of society in which technologies, requirements and structures are under constant change. In contemporary society, entrepreneurship can be said to be a generator of innovation and development. The results achieved by the entrepreneur lead to a creative destruction of competence – *the entrepreneur as the creative destroyer of equilibrium.*[4]

Entrepreneurship is problem orientated to the extent that new knowledge and opportunism bring change to the economic system. You might say that the entrepreneur is like the marine parallel to the proverbial cat among the pigeons, the catfish in the floating tank: a force that by its own enterprising movements keeps the water free of ice, ensures water circulation and oxygen supply, thus creating living conditions for itself as well as others.

For a moment, think about innovative companies like Intel (technological competence), Microsoft (market understanding), McDonald's (disciplined management concept) or 3Com with the PDA concept Palm (unique customer empathy). Now sparkling stars and global market leaders each in their own field. From the start, microscopic, new entrants disrupting the existing equilibrium in well established industries, dominated by large-scale corporations who were, incidentally, themselves trying to conquer the new markets while keeping others out, or who remained content as long as their own existing positions could not be threatened. Born by enterprise with an ability to see what others had

---

4   Wickman (1998) referring to Schumpeter. "The task of the entrepreneur is creative destruction". Kirzner (1974): "The entrepreneur is someone who is alert to profitable opportunities for exchange", Deakins David and Fred Mark (2003): "The Cantillon entrepreneur brings people, money and materials together to create an entirely new organization = the classic type of entrepreneur who identifies an unexploited opportunity and then innovates in order to pursue it …. Their innovation is so important that a whole industry is created on its back …". Wickman (1998): "Disruption of equilibrium can be perceived as the dynamic creation of equilibrium".

overlooked. And, in addition, focusing on understanding problems and the real reasons for them.[5]

Ansoff (1987)[6] contrasts entrepreneurial culture with the more usual continual organisational behaviour in the following way: "Instead of striving to maintain and consolidate the past, the entrepreneurial organisation constantly strives to change status quo". Thus Ansoff recognises that the core of entrepreneurship is constant readiness for change and market orientation

Successful entrepreneurial launching requires special knowledge. Knowledge in the best and broadest sense is a prerequisite for sustainable development of ideas and accordingly for efficient entrepreneurship.

The argument can also be turned around. Ultimately, the value of knowledge will depend on whether it can be used to create new opportunities. It would be reasonable to claim that a modern economy with its demand for ever higher volumes and speed in the cycle of development is not only an *economy based on knowledge*, but can also – and perhaps in particular – be seen as an *economy based on ideas* in the specific sense that the need and demand for more new sustainable ideas grows very swiftly. This is partly the result of hyper-competition. When the cycle of change grows ever shorter, whether in connection with norms, materials, process technology, costs structures, etc., competitive pressure will grow exponentially.[7]

Financially sustainable ideas rarely arrive as a result of a stroke of genius or by mere chance, although luck, coincidence, ambition and intuition are necessary attributes. Nor do sustainable ideas automatically follow in the wake of new, important, scientific discoveries or technological advances and sweeping change. Entrepreneurship very much has to do with being systematic and fostering *interaction* between special competencies embedded in a target-oriented course of events.

---

5 Afuah (1998) explains the Henderson-Clark model which distinguishes between four types of innovation: (1) regular, (2) niche, (3) revolutionary and (4) architectural. Architectural innovations breaks down the technical competencies of existing companies as well as their market competencies. For this reason, it is extremely difficult for them to acquire these competencies.

6 As well as Hills et alt (1994).

7 D'Aveni (1995) on hyper-competition: "There are revolutions in quality that raise standards and then new revolutions that shatter those standards. There are innovations in product and process technology that drive dramatic improvements in quality or reductions in cost. These cycles of change are growing progressively shorter. Advances in information, manufacturing, and basic technology have accelerated so quickly that many processes and products now have lives of three months or less before they become obsolete".

1.2 Who becomes an entrepreneur?

Is it possible to speak of a special entrepreneurial personality? Some say yes. They claim that only certain extraordinary personalities are capable of creating major changes – in other words, that entrepreneurs constitute a special tribe within the population. Others believe that the great, creative personality types have typically undergone special difficulties in fitting in socially, they have been excluded, have not had enough paternal attention, acceptance or other things along those lines, and have chosen the path of entrepreneurship motivated by a deep, subconscious need for recognition, and have achieved the competency and energy by refusing to obey the norms of society. The evidence supporting this portrayal seems farfetched and inconsistent with general observations. People who choose to become entrepreneurs are generally optimists – they believe in opportunities, they think in terms of what can be done. They generally enjoy a fairly high level of self-assurance, but it is unlikely that they represent a special psycho-social segment of their own.

Nor, contrary to popular opinion, do entrepreneurs go in search of risk, and they do not dream of their businesses becoming instant successes. Drucker (1986) puts it like this:"Those entrepreneurs who start up with the idea that they will make it big – and in a hurry – can be guaranteed failure. They are almost bound to do the wrong things. An innovation that looks big may turn out to be no more than technical virtuosity; an innovation with moderate intellectual pretension, a McDonald's for instance may turn into gigantic, highly profitable business".

The point being that entrepreneurship can be *learned,* and that to a large extent, coincidence determines who will start up a business of their own. Entrepreneurship is a way of thinking, a way of acting, a form of organising, not a personal quality reserved for a minority of the population: entrepreneurship is a social construction which arises in the interaction between people in certain situations, professional connections and life phases. This viewpoint fully recognises the importance of talent, determination and individual competencies.

The essence of entrepreneurship is to have a *different perception of a given situation.* As an entrepreneur you can see what might be, and not just what actually is – you have the ability to glimpse future relations between factors that may create new value and new opportunities.

---

8   Wickman (1998), Hills (1974), Drucker (1986).

Entrepreneurship presupposes the presence of performance motivation, a competitive mindset characterised by ambition, insight, diligence and self-confidence – but is that really so unique?

1.3 The basic competencies of the entrepreneurial process

Business initiatives differ in character. On the surface, the business which requires a purely competency driven research and development process has not much in common with distinctly market orientated innovation for which the decisive success criterion is being able to put your ear to the ground and understand customers. One initiative focuses on solution-orientated creation of knowledge and experiments, while the other concentrates on understanding customer problems and needs. One seems to be introverted the other extroverted. But they both have their eye on the creation of opportunities; they both contain a combination of analysis and creativity. They both look for what has not yet been explored – for what is surprising. As a result, in general, the birth of a sustainable business initiative requires the presence of three well defined types of core competencies in an entrepreneurial organisation in the earliest phase. The competencies are called the three Graces:

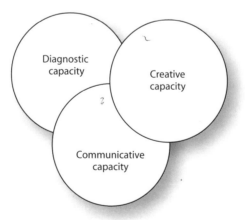

Figure 1.1 The three Graces in the birth of a business initiative[9]

---

9   Levitt (1983) distinguishes between visionary, analytical and purposeful forces.

Diagnosis, creativity and communication come together as competencies of equal value in the early, amoebic phases of business initiatives. This means that team play is the be all and end all of the game. Team play requires an awareness of the preferred professional and cooperative role of the individual players.

Initiatives that fail further down the line are characterised either by insufficient competency at the birth of the project – or, more frequently – by insufficient balance *between* the three Graces. Possibly because a charismatic, over-enthusiastic entrepreneur-champion underestimates the importance of the human factor or the relevance of sublime market insight. Or because the project runs into paralysis by analysis, the fact that such high analytical demands have been made to the decision-making basis that, paradoxically, the outcome is an inability to act, something which will of course eventually kill off the leadership which is, in any event, necessary to create momentum.

The art consists in giving each of the three Graces enough room for manoeuvre while, at the same time, ensuring interaction between them – which leads to collective learning and, thus, to better chances of success.

Most would-be entrepreneurs do not stumble – they give up before they start. However, if we choose to view the birth of the venture more as a team effort than as a solo performance, many of us will find that we possess a distinct role profile of strength which fits admirably into the competency picture provided that all the other roles in the venture have been cast with a similar level of competence.

1.4 Entrepreneurship as a process

In principle a business venture can start in two different ways: with a *problem orientation* or with a *solution orientation*,[10] in which the former is synonymous with market need, and the second with a product or technological breakthrough. In a concrete business venture, a market focus and a competence focus are not contradictory factors, but business ventures can be categorised as one or the other as far as their origin is concerned. The two types of ventures encounter very different challenges, and for that reason they are exposed to highly different developmental conditions in the early phase of the project life.

---

10 Hence a distinction is made between perception = problem orientation and conception = solution orientation. This distinction may be criticised for being mechanistic.

The *problem orientated* form of business venture starts with the discovery of an unsolved problem of a sufficient magnitude, and an awareness of the fact that a solution to that problem represents value.[11] Ventures based on understanding a problem – market insight – have a better chance of succeeding. The reason for this is terribly simple. Problems indicate a need that has not been met and thus a business opportunity. Furthermore, focusing on problems reflects definite customer and market orientation in which strong sensitivity is combined with a highly developed interpretative ability. This is a cultural feature in the project which not only creates value in the start-up phase, but also later in the project life whenever new needs, segments, distribution channels, etc., arise.

It must be emphasised that it is not enough to discover that something is a problem. Only when the roots of the problem can be described in an unconventional and innovative manner, and when they can be concretely changed into an opportunity will the idea attain economic value and only then will it make sense. Many unsolved problems are not important enough and, therefore, do not contain an embedded business opportunity.

Aluminium drip catchers for wine bottles, to prevent stains on your tablecloth or your jacket, solve a simple, trivial problem – wine bottles will drip when wine is poured. It is easy to explain and equally easy to remedy with an efficient and affordable solution. The rare feature here was the ability to actualise the opportunity by seeing the problem in a new, different way.

Conversely, problems than can only be explained in abstract, conventional terms – for example, the mysteries of cancer or congested motorways – do not contain the seed of a business venture, unless the root causes can be described specifically, coherently, innovatively and related to an opportunity.

Often, customers do not know that they have a problem, or else they have grown accustomed to the discrepancy between the actual situation and the possible situation: dripping wine bottles, vacuum cleaner bags that have to be changed, congestion on the motorway, and the like. Problem orientated entrepreneurship has to do with knowing more about what customers need than they do themselves – and then to know why. Business initiatives that are born by the discovery of a problem should not be judged from a static point of view: what might customers be missing at the moment? Entrepreneurship is dynamic, driven by imagination, forward looking, combinatory and upward striving: if it was possible, would it entail value for the customer if .... The fact that every

---

11 Seen from this angle, entrepreneurship can be considered an information discipline.

home was missing the incandescent lamp was not the problem addressed by Thomas Edison, but the notion that it would create gigantic value, if one day it were to be technically and financially possible.

The entrepreneurial process can also use as its point of departure a *solution*, typically a technology, a process, a new material or a combination of them. The entrepreneurial task in the solution based venture typically has to do with commercialising scientific results expressed in questions such as, "How can this conception solve a problem in a better or less costly way than the ones that already exist?" Trail-blazing business ideas are often created by new technical possibilities. However, the entrepreneurial process may be difficult for the solution orientated business venture, because it often presupposes that customers will change their pattern of use or purchasing habits, and there are not many suppliers to stimulate demand.

As we all know, cows do not give us milk, it has to be taken from them. The same applies to business opportunities: they are not discovered, they are *created*. Entrepreneurship is a trade, not a detection effort. This contention does not attempt to settle a theoretical discussion about an opportunity – an incongruity – is latently present, only waiting to be discovered by an alert entrepreneur, or whether it is this specific combination of factors in the business venture itself that is the prerequisite for the conception and realisation of the opportunity.

The statement: that the precondition for profitable entrepreneurial activities are (exclusively) found where people do not know what it is that they do not know, and do not know that they do not know it, is tempting and plausible. And what has been overlooked does not have to be subtle, mysterious or complicated. Often the most obvious things are those that are most overlooked.

1.5 Invention, innovation and entrepreneurship

The concepts of invention, innovation and entrepreneurship are sometimes confused:

Invention – and the discoveries behind inventions – is an idea without any immediate commercial value, until someone develops an application and introduces it to the market. The steam engine, electricity or the microprocessor were inventions, but they only became valuable with the development of applications: the steam driven locomotive, the incandescent lamp, electronic products. Applications stimulate demand. Business ventures based on spectacular inventions may be extremely difficult to realise successfully because they require drastic changes among customers. In nearly every respect, railways were technically and financially superior to canals and horse driven transport, but it was a new application, strong vested interests worked against it, and it could not rely on any network effect. For a long time, gas illumination companies tried to disseminate doubt about the usefulness and safety of the incandescent lamp, and they were successful.

Often, breakthroughs do not arrive painlessly despite their obvious usefulness. Perhaps there is a shortage of competitors to stimulate demand as a result of intellectual property rights. Or perhaps the buyers hold back because of the new product being incompatible with other products or habits. Furthermore, the success of the invention will depend on the acceptance of the mass market – a high ambition, indeed.

The term invention refers to the company's achievement of technical perfection and the new production methods linked to it as an objective in itself.

Innovation refers to the endeavours of a company to introduce new products, methods, processes, materials, etc.[12] aimed at the market. Whereas the critical success factor for an invention is technical, it is commercial for an innovation. The bridge between invention and innovation consists in the entrepreneurial competency of the organisation, the group or the individual.

An innovation is the *way* in which to do something differently, less costly or better. Therefore, innovation can be seen both as a thing and as a process of renewal.

We may distinguish between radical and incremental innovation. *Radical innovations* are new fundamental technologies and logics that trigger many derived, smaller innovations and allow man special scopes of application. These are the trailblazing ideas that change the world and lead to a shift in paradigms – push-innovations.[13] One such example is the microprocessor which today is used in virtually all relations and products/markets.

---

12 Hills (1994) et alt. Sundbo (2001, 2002).

13 *Paradigms* suggest units of analysis, constructs and similar necessary elements to form evaluation techniques within a specific discipline, basically, that is the reason why they are so relevant. Yet paradigms fall short of advancing propositions, axioms, lawlike generalisations and testable hypotheses. Paradigms are not theories.

Incremental innovations are smaller, market initiated innovations for which impulses from customers, increasing fragmentation of needs over the product life cycle or competitors' moves create pressures for renewal and adjustment.[14]

Henry Ford's revolutionary production principle – the assembly line – was an innovation which, in reality, was not nearly as much technology push as market pull. Ford saw the opportunity to sell cars to a mass market provided the price was low enough, and on the basis of this recognition he created a completely different business concept anchored in a new logistical system. Ingvar Kamrad's IKEA was created on the basis of the same type of market innovation: good quality furniture for ordinary people, supported by a well run network-driven supply chain.

Innovation must be seen as the knowledge basis for *entrepreneurship*. Somewhat simplified we can say that entrepreneurship constitutes the financial and managerial driving force within the framework of which innovation will take place. Therefore, entrepreneurship is the opportunity to do something in a different, less costly and better way.

Only a tiny fraction of new business ventures get off the ground; most fail before and during the start or perish when competitive pressures grow, because of technological shifts in paradigm or along the road of industry consolidation. The infancy of the motor industry is a clear case in point:

The horseless carriage

The structure of the motor industry in its early years was instable in each and every respect. The entry barriers were relatively low. The technological barrier was simply the ability to design and manufacture a car consisting of purchased components. Perhaps not a simple task – but, nevertheless, this was achievable

---

14 There are many differing typologies applied to innovation, i.e. Martin (1994) (1) Revolutionary, radical technology. Discontinuity, competence destroying. (2) Micro radical. Competence enhancing. (3) Incremental puzzle solving. Normal technological innovation. Innovation: Conception + invention + exploitation. Referring to Tushman and Roenkopf, Afuah (1998) distinguishes between four stages in the technological life cycle: (1) Technological discontinuity, (2) Era of ferment, (3) Era of dominant design, and (4) Era of incremental change. Another typology: (1) Regular innovations conserve the firm's existing capabilities, (2) Niche innovations preserve technological capabilities, but make market capabilities obsolete, (3) Revolutionary innovations preserve market capabilities but destroy technological capabilities and (4) Architectural innovations – here both types of capabilities are destroyed.

for many people. Car manufacture was still in its infancy, and the process was, essentially, one of assembling parts. It was a period of relative favourable economic conditions and ample access to capital. As long as a motor car could be produced to order, and as long as your creditors would grant you credit, the need for venture capital and operating capital was a surmountable barrier. In an industry which was growing and attracting attention, it was on the cards that it would attract many entrepreneurs. In the USA alone, more than 500 firms were established in a period of ten years. Interestingly, during this period, there were a lot of establishments as well as closures.

The first 18 car manufacturers in the USA accounted for 80% of total output. This concentration remained unchanged for quite some time, but, please, note the following: firstly, the number of suppliers was reduced as a result of consolidations and bankruptcies. Secondly, other companies replaced most of the top 20 companies. It was only when demand grew over the next decade that the top positions became fairly stable. So whereas conditions rather favoured invaders – new business ventures – they did not favour stability. The financial foundations of most of the firms were extremely fragile and could quickly send shockwaves through the industry whenever business conditions fluctuated.

Despite these clear danger signals, the industry attracted a lot of players during the first decade of the 20th century. Despite the fact that the top 10 producers on the eastern seaboard of the USA accounted for 70% of sales, their market position was still insufficiently anchored, and the market itself was too underdeveloped to provide any market leadership.

In 1907 the price of an average car was $3,700 corresponding to $212,000 in present-day prices. This corresponds to the price of a luxury yacht. Even after the introduction of the Model T and the growth of the mass market, prices remained relatively high compared to today's standards. In 1916 the price of an average car was $1,000 corresponding to approximately $45,000 today – although the cheapest models were only half that price.

At the time, the elimination race was well under way, and the image of who were going to be the long-term winners and losers was very clear. Out of the top 10 manufacturers of 1915 only three were not among the top 10 ten years later. The market had not become more concentrated as the top 20 manufacturers had always accounted for 80% of sales. The thing was that the number of exits grew while, at the same time, the entrance barriers were also raised leading to a reduction of new entrants.

Today, only Ford and GM are still with us. Who remembers Studebaker, Packard or Winton?

The story of the early childhood of the motorcar reveals how few the winners are and how many will be losers in the selection process in new industries. Coincidences, alertness, cynicism, empathy and vision are all necessary, if not sufficient, preconditions for becoming a successful pioneer. In some ways, the example is reminiscent of the hyperactivity of e-commerce activities around the turn of the millennium, a time when it was possible to obtain risk capital for everything that smelled of Internet-trade or dotcom, all the way from lingerie to dog collars. Only, the cycle was swifter, more vigorous and attracted even more entrepreneurs; losses were many times higher and left the world seriously hung over and in a deeply contemplative mood.

Apart from generalities, there are no universally valid explanations of why business ventures fail, except for the fact that new lucrative markets will always attract far more business ventures than the long term opportunities can sustain. So when industry consolidation sets in, a large majority of firms will roll over and die. It also remains an incontestable fact that new businesses will fold if nobody wants to buy their products.

1.6 Inventory: Entrepreneurial motives and competencies

Entrepreneurship has to do with opportunities and, therefore, with people. As pointed out above, noone has so far been able to show that entrepreneurs constitute a tribe unto themselves, or that they possess special, recurrent, significant mental traits. They are as different from each other as they are from other people. Nature and nurture do not create entrepreneurs anymore than they create other career paths. Sometimes the son is like his father – at other times he is not. And as the chapter says, entrepreneurship is created through collective efforts and role differentiation.

Therefore, many people may be possible-entrepreneurs. If certain personal or professional circumstances or special conditions in the surrounding world arise – dangers or opportunities – potential entrepreneurs will choose to take part in new business ventures.

Below you will find an inventory for self-analysis. This inventory allows the individual to analyse herself in relation to central issues in connection with entrepreneurship: readiness, preferred role, competence, goals and motivation, limitations, attitude to risk, etc.

The analytical diagram should not be seen as a personality profile test to be graded and interpreted unambiguously. Nevertheless, the analysis may give you a hint and can be used as a basis for dialogue in a project team to establish strength profiles and attitudes:

In the following diagram you will find a number of observations concerning the motives and competencies of entrepreneurs, subdivided into categories. How well does each observation fit you? Each observation is rated between 1 and 10 depending on how well you think the observation fits you, the better it fits, the more points you will assign to it. You may only use 10 points for each category. If, for example, a single observation really fits you compared to the others in that category, you should give it ten points and all the others should get 0. If you recognise yourself in several observations, you should distribute the points accordingly. Be spontaneous and honest.

	OBSERVATION	POINTS	COMMENTS
I	**Category: Independence.** **As a entrepreneur, I would prefer**		
A	Making my hobby into my business and my living		
B	Switching from being an employee to being an independent consultant		
C	Purchasing an existing business		
D	Becoming a franchise taker or similar		
E	Starting my own business because of my "entrepreneurial spirit"		
F	Finding a match between my competency and a market potential		
G	Developing a vision and realising an idea		
H	Total	10	

II	Category: My goals as self-employed. As an entrepreneur an important goal for me would be:		
A	To be financially independent		
B	To make my own decisions		
C	To earn a lot of money		
D	To create an important firm		
E	To be the one to start a whole new industry		
F	To gain recognition		
G	To realise my own idea for idealistic reasons		
H	Total	10	
III	Push and pull impulses that might make me an entrepreneur:		
A	Suddenly catching sight of a business idea		
B	Actually making an invention		
C	My executive career developing disappointingly		
D	Being made redundant and not being able to find a job		
E	Running into somebody who had a good idea		
F	Being able to capitalise on my own knowledge		
G	My education or profession indicates that direction		
H	Total	10	

IV	Attitude to risk.		
	In my considerations, these risks would play a decisive role		
A	I would be sacrificing a promising career as an employee		
B	My self-confidence would suffer severely if the project failed		
C	Not wanting to reduce my family's standard of living during the start-up phase		
D	Not risking losing my home		
E	Ending up with a considerable debt afterwards		
F	Not being able to get a job if things do not work out		
G	Not having the support and understanding of all the family		
H	Total	10	
V	My preferred role in the entrepreneurial process.		
	I can add the most value by:		
A	Being the creative force; the one who gets the ideas		
B	Being the analytical type, finding and processing the facts		
C	Mediating good cooperation, building bridges between people		
D	Creating a strong external network		
E	Organising processes taking them forward in a logical order		
F	Putting things into practice		
G	Keeping spirits high in the entire team		
H	Total	10	

VI	Form of working with in entrepreneurship. My way of working is characterised by:		
A	Enjoying hard work		
B	Definitely being a self-starter		
C	Having considerable confidence in myself		
D	Being sensitive and eager to learn		
E	Being a fairly robust type who does not give up easily		
F	Being turned on by competition		
G	Having high personal goals		
H	Total	10	
VII	Limitations in terms of entrepreneurship. As a self-employed person, my limitations would be:		
A	My professional competence is not yet high enough; I am too young		
B	My professional competence is too old and 'rusty' for these requirements		
C	The barriers to entry in the industries I know are too high		
D	If I do take this step, all the career doors would close behind me		
E	It is difficult to find the right idea-opportunity		
F	The personal costs and risks are too high		
G	I do not think I am suited to it		
H	Total	10	

	The observations in the categories I-VII that fit me the best as an entrepreneur are:		
I			
II			
III			
IV			
V			
VI			
VII			

Entrepreneurial motives and competencies

The battery of questions is aimed at a qualitative, individual assessment exclusively. In addition, the profile can form the basis for balancing attitudes and expectations in a group moving towards entrepreneurship and may contribute to outlining the contours of the group profile vis-à-vis the basic competencies of the entrepreneurial project.

Literature

Afuah: *Innovation Management – Strategies, Implementation and profits.* N.Y. Oxford University Press 1998.

Ansoff Igor: *Corporate Strategy.* Penguin Books. London. 1987.

Bird Barbara J: *Entrepreneurial Behaviour.* Scott Foresman & Co. 1989.

Bridge Simon O'Neill and Cromie Scran*: Understanding Enterprise, Entrepreneurship and Small Business.* Palgrave MacMillan N.Y. 1998.

Carson David et alt.: *Marketing and Entrepreneurship in SME's – an innovative approach.* Prentice Hall. N.Y. US 1995.

CESFO: *The Global Entrepreneurship Monitor.* Danish National Report 2002.

D'Aveni Richard A: *Hypercompetitive Rivalries – Competition in Highly Dynamic Environments.* The Free Press. N.Y. USA 1995.

Deakins David, Freel Mark: *Entrepreneurship and small Firms*. Mc.Graw Hill Education 2003.

Det Økonomiske Råds Formandskab: *Dansk Økonomi. Forår 2003*. Kapitel VII: "Entrepreneurskab og Venturekapital". 2003.

Drucker Peter F. *Innovation and Entrepreneurship – practice and principles*. Butterworth, London. 1986 (1999).

Drucker Peter F.: *The Discipline of Innovation*. Harvard Business Review, Nov-Dec 1998 s 149 – 156.

EVCA: *The Global Competitiveness Report*. 2002.

FORA (Økonomi- og Erhvervsministeriet): *Et benchmark studie af iværksætteraktivitet – hvad kan Danmark lære*. 2002.

Franklin Carl: *Why innovations fail*. Spiro Press. London. 2003.

Gren Svendsen, Pløger Lillian: *Generationsskifte i små og mellemstore virksomheder*. Center for Småvirksomhedsforskning, CESFO. Syddansk Universitet. Kolding. 2000.

Harper David A.: *Entrepreneurship and the market process*. Rothledge. London. 1996.

Herlau Henrik, Tetzschner Helge: *Fra jobtager til jobmager*. Samfundslitteratur. 2. udgave 1999.

Hills Gerald et alt: *Marketing and entrepreneurship research – ideas and opportunities*. Quorum books. Greenwood Press Weestport. Connecticut, US. 1994.

Hougaard Søren og Bjerre Mogens: *Strategic Relationship Marketing*. Samfundslitteratur Press. Copenhagen 2002.

Iværksætteren Nummer 3, september 2003. København. 2003.

Kirzner Israel M.: *Competition and Entrepreneurship*. University of Chicago Press. Chicago. US. 1974.

Kuhn T.S: The structure of scientific revolutions. University of Chicago Presse. 1970

Levitt: *Marketing Imagination*. N.Y. 1983.

Lundström Anders, Stevenson Lois: *On the Road to Entrepreneurship* Policy. Vol 1. Elanders Gotap. 2002.

Martin Michael JC: *Managing Innovation and Entrepreneurship in Technology Based Firms*. John Wiley & Sons. 1994.

Nairn Alasdair: *Engines moving Markets*. Wiley & Sons. N.Y. 2002.

Nielsen Orla og Wilke Ricky: *Organisationers købsadfærd i grundtræk*. Samfundslitteratur. 1999.

Pearson Alan W. Ed. By Henry Jane, Walker David: *Managing Innovation: An Uncertainty Reduction process*. Sage Publications. London. UK. 1991.

Schumpeter Joseph: *Capitalism, Socialism and Democracy*. Harper & Row. N.Y. 1934.

Schumpeter Joseph: *Entrepreneurship and Innovation*. Entrepreneurship. 2000.

Sundbo Jon, Fuglsang Lars, Norvig Larsen Jacob: *Innovation med omtanke*. Systime. 2001.

Sundbo Jon: *The Strategic Management of Innovation. A sociological and Economic Theory*. Elgar Publishing Limited. UK. 2002.

Times Jeff. A.: *New Venture Creation – Entrepreneurship for the 21.st Century*. Mc. Graw Hill. 1990.

Vækstfonden: *Benchmarking af markedet for innovationsfinansiering*. 2003.

Wickman Philip A: *A Decision making Approach to New Venture Creation and Management*. Pitman Publishing. London. 1998.

2. Creative market insight

"A moment's insight is sometimes worth a life's experience."
Oliver Wendell Holmes 1809-94

Empathy with customer needs is the primary, crucial condition for the success of a new business venture. The unsurpassable product idea can rarely muster the same competitive force as a concept originating in creative market understanding[15]. The function of the entrepreneur is precisely to uncover what has been overlooked. The view that without any profound insight into the market – no viable business seems to be so self-evident that it is surprising that entrepreneurs seem to underestimate this very aspect. Possibly, conceptual things are more fascinating than perceptual ones. Perhaps it is more motivating to think about a product idea and a functional possibility than to trace a need and see the world through the eyes of customers?

Chapter 2 supplies a frame of reference for developing creative market understanding concentrating on four themes that have been called the Four-Leaf-Clover Model, viz. occurrences, incongruities, innovations and missing links. Establishing a flexible, conceptual platform requires an analytical approach and imagination. Creative market understanding is definitely the first step on the way towards formulating new, viable business ideas.

2.1 Solution versus problem orientation

Many business ideas are biased from the start; they suffer from market orientation vitamin deficiency. Apparently, *conceptual enthusiasm* tends to overshadow

---

15 Drucker (1986) endorses this point, "For all the visibility, glamour and importance of science-based innovation, it is actually the least reliable and the least predictable one". Franklin (2003) refers to a study in which researchers analysed 197 product innovations out of which 111 had been successful, while 86 had failed. The study concludes that the successful innovations had one or more of the following features: they were moderately new to the market, based on known and tested technology; they allowed customers to save money and supported existing patterns of behaviour. Reversely, the failed innovations were based on new, untested technology.

perceptual empathy. In the classic situation the entrepreneur is standing there with his finished, trailblazing, new product that nobody wants.

A comprehensive study[16] of successful business ventures supports this contention. The study showed that most successes were derived from market needs, and that only 20% originated in a product idea or a service. We must, of course, be careful not to over-interpret such success/failure studies of which there are many. It is possible that more market innovative and market imitative ventures are launched than technological ones. Perhaps the successful tech companies are more successful than others when, finally, they do succeed, because the concept is bigger. Nevertheless, it is thought-provoking that the market perspective is always stressed as *the* central criterion for success.

The inventive venture Infra

Windows always open outward. This is the building tradition in Denmark. Outward opening windows can sometimes be quite impractical in high-rise and multi-storey buildings, for instance when they are to be cleaned. Either you have to lean out while clasping the window bar, something which is quite hazardous to do on the 5th floor. Or you have to hire a window cleaner who uses a ladder or a lift to clean your windows – quite a costly affair.

In one fell swoop the Infra window was to solve this problem. The construction, which was patented, consisted, among other things (but not exclusively) of a paradigm shift from opening outward to opening inward – a stroke of genius, apparently. The product was developed at a time when most of the housing stock was about to have the original windows replaced. A series of market interviews was carried out with the people living in flats as informants. Generally they were very keen on the idea, and the analyses unambiguously showed that there was a considerable market for the new product. The idea never became a hit, but completely faded away. It ran into massive opposition – indeed, it was barely taken seriously – from architects, engineers and public authorities for completely different reasons than those having to do with window cleaning

---

16 Henry and Walker, ed. (1991) includes 567 innovations. Furthermore Henry and Walker refer to Globe's study of ten radical innovations, Project Sappho. The project covered 43 projects grouped in pairs – one success one failure, and 41 variables proved significant for the outcome of the project. The most important ones were: (1) understanding customer needs, (2) attention to marketing and PR, (3) development efficiency, (4) efficient exploitation of external technology and scientific discoveries and (5) managerial experience and know-how.

and user friendliness, which allegedly was to be given no special priority over construction criteria like aesthetics, safety and tradition. And who, if we are honest, is the real boss and decision maker and, thus, the customer, when it is a question of new windows in a multi-storey building? Mrs Jenkins on the 5th floor or the technicians .....?

The Infra window was technically sophisticated and the point of the need was well taken, however, the company had the wrong focus in relation to the critical points of the value and decision making chain.

It would be fair to claim that behind any innovative product idea or invention there is always a well-considered supposition that the design will solve a particular problem for particular users: a need exists and that the creative feeling for needs is exactly the distinctive mark of the skilful inventor.

And that is often how things really are. The problem as seen by the innovator raring to go, is very quickly to arrive at what you might call the *market conclusion affirming the solution*. As soon as it is thought that the problem for the customers has been identified and the idea has been conceived – the riddle solved – the problem perception is frozen, and attention is shifted from market insight towards the far more riveting activity of developing the concept – focus is moved from cognition to design. This entails a risk of rigidity in the venture, and therefore a risk of deficiency in market acceptance further down the line. To be had: Solution. Wanted: Problem. Drucker (1986), for instance, stresses time and again that because entrepreneurial problems seem ill structured, entrepreneurship does not start with an attempt to solve a problem, but with an attempt to define the problem and to assess why it is a genuine problem. Microsound used problem orientation as its point of departure.

The story of Søren Louis Pedersen

"You are mumbling, I can't hear you!"
Søren Louis Pedersen is an engineer and one of the world's greatest developers of hearing aids. He has had a brilliant career at Oticon, the global market leader and had been one of the key people behind the technical development of the world's first digital hearing aid which, when launched, provided Oticon (William Demant) stock with dramatically higher values on the stock market.

Some years and a few jobs after the Oticon years, Søren decided to go it alone. One would have thought that as a brilliant engineer and head-designer

Søren would get to grips with high tech inventions or the like. But, no. Instead he wanted to be the one to create a global market for hearing-aid spectacles.

He knew that an ever growing part of the population (mainly men) suffer from impaired hearing. So much so, that they find it difficult to hear what is said in large assemblies or groups, on television, in rooms with a lot of background noise and poor acoustics, and the like. In short, an annoying and increasing inability for more and more people.

The threshold you have to overcome before you acquire a hearing aid and recognise the complaint and the fact that you have become a patient, is fairly high. This occurs as to many people, a hearing aid signals old age, and because the acquisition and the adjustment of the aid to the individual customer takes place in an environment of white coats, as with all other types of medical aids (apart from spectacles). Many people suffer from a chronic medical complaint, but for psychological reasons they reject the solution offered by the hearing aid industry and the medical sector.

Søren founded Microsound Inc. because he was convinced that those with a slight hearing impairment are ready to wear a personal communication device, if it looks like a cordless headset, can by bought like any other product and can be individually adjusted according to the do-it-yourself method. In early 2003, Microsound launched the cordless "headset". A Pilot with an accompanying Eartuner in cooperation with one of Europe's leading optician chains … Microsound is looking to introduce an entirely new product category based on empathic insight into very specific needs.

To Microsound, the question is in what the customer's problem consists. Microsound addresses a positioning problem – the idea that a new product concept can change people's perception of a hearing aid from being an aid to being a snazzy headset. A few generations ago, spectacles too were considered an aid; today spectacles are a positive part of an individual's look, governed by fashion and by the occasion in which they are worn, although many people prefer contact lenses or even a laser-beam operation. Microsound saw and understood a problem which everyone had, so far, just put up with.

2.2 The Four-Leaf-Clover Model

Creative market insight and tracing market opportunities are the results of an analytical-creative process. Finding the needle in the haystack does not only require knowing what a needle looks like, but also that you search in a particular way. Creative market insight is not identical with gifted market analysis. It takes more – i.e., surprise and new ways of thinking beyond what is usual. Questions that lead to creative market insight have to be concrete, such as: New cars have central locks with remote control. Why not have a remote control for locks to houses? Or: Would it not be possible to give brown bread a designer label just like coffee or cheese? Why should we put up with dripping wine bottles? Or: What a bother it is to change the bag of the vacuum cleaner. Is it really necessary?

In *The Business Idea* we shall take up and discuss four main roads towards the goal of creative market insight, and hence to the fountainhead of business opportunities. Below, these four roads will be called the Four-Leaf Clover, see Figure 2.1 below.[17] These are roads that can be travelled and explored systematically. Follow, stop, charter for rules, traffic and danger signals.

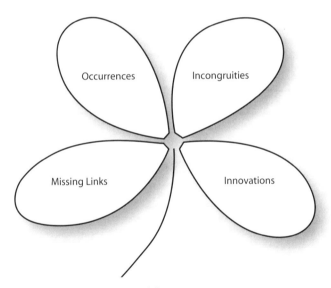

Figure 2.1 The Four-Leaf Clover Model

---

17 Mullins (2006) operates with the following opportunity types and thus the way forward to creative market insight: 1. opportunities originating in macro trends, 2. Opportunities originating in experiencing and understanding customer problems, 3. Opportunities originating in scientific results, 4. Opportunities documented within other sectors and capable of being transferred. Franklin (2003) goes a step further and uses the concept of idea factor, for instance, identification of need, identification of application, mental inventions and random moments.

Anyone who has ever tried to find a four-leaf clover knows that it takes a great deal of luck, but that one of the prerequisites for this kind of luck is that you kneel down on a lawn or in a field and carefully search an area where there is a lot of clover. If you keep on your feet, chances of finding one are infinitesimal. Therefore, four-leave clovers are not only associated with good luck and fortune, but also with detailed investigation.

Together, occurrences, incongruities, missing links and innovations constitute the road network of market creativity. They are not common market analysis themes or concepts; they include orientation according to needs and opportunities. They search for changes, non-optimal situations, unpractical features and new knowledge. They contain potential magical moments.

Uncovering problems in the market has to do with identifying what values the customer might possibly be in the market for – the same as an impulse for a business opportunity. We might call this impulse *the external source*. An alternative approach would be to base ourselves on the entrepreneur's actual or sought for competencies: what is it that I can do and want to do and, based on that, track down areas where these abilities can unfold – *the internal source*.[18]

Occurrences and innovations are *sudden changes*[19] leading to unpractical features that are relevant and topical for a problem, need or possible value for potential customers. Incongruities and missing links constitute *latent unpractical features* waiting to be discovered and remedied in an industry, a customer segment, a process or the like.

Note that the four-leaf-clover model compresses all external changes, disruptions to the economic climate, including interest levels, that are of crucial relevance to investment calculations and, therefore, to the sustainability of ideas,

---

18 Internal versus external sources for creating competitive advantages reflects the inside-out versus the outside-in discussion. Theoretically the two perspectives are each other's antithesis and are based on different notions of whether lasting competitive advantages (given that they even exist in a hyper-competitive world) can be anchored in resource immobility (= specific competencies) or exclusively in an ability to react to change faster/better than the competitors (structure-conduct-performance) which causes a barrier to go up. The discussion between the two lines of thought and counter-poles is lively with strong adherents on either side; however it seems unending and fundamentally unproductive.

19 Mullins (2003) emphasises that there are, "attractive markets" and "lousy markets". Changes that give rise to entrepreneurial opportunities rarely lead to success if the market happens to be a lousy one despite all the entrepreneur's ability.

under the heading *Occurrences* which, systematically, draws attention to what has been overlooked, what is sudden and to future trends.

We shall now look at the leaves of the four-leaf clover in further detail.

2.3 Occurrences in a diagnostic perspective

An overwhelming number of successful new business ideas exploit change. Of course, ideas do exist that in and of themselves *constitute* drastic change, but these are the exceptions. Consequently, a systematic scrutiny of areas characterised by change, typically offering opportunities for new entrepreneurial activity, is essential.

The term "occurrences" has been consciously chosen over the word "change" which is normally applied to phenomena triggering new threat and opportunity images in management and strategy literature. Occurrences are a *special* type of change: sudden, or overlooked, subject to dissemination over time and place, providing a chance of gaining a lead or unique interpretation – the germ of business ideas. Sometimes even taking the form of paranoid notions.

Occurrences carry a shimmer of discovery – thinking by jumps and leaps, asymmetrical knowledge, hidden value, optimal timing. When occurrences are disseminated and integrated into established decision making systems they gradually lose their potential as fountainheads for understanding problems and entrepreneurial initiatives.

Unexpected events may lead to new needs and prepare the ground for new business ventures. Here what springs to mind is not just natural catastrophes, epidemics, disasters, wars, new legislation, etc., creating demand and thereby business opportunities for agile and creative entrepreneurs. Unexpected events can also come in the form of successes, failures or external events, which might put you on the trail of a differentiated market insight, for complementary products or substitutes or completely unrelated services.

After the terror attack on the Twin Towers of the World Trade Center in New York, on 11 September 2001, the market for taxi and chartered flights flourished because passengers grew wary of travelling with the big air carriers. By contrast, the expected intense increase in the market for equipment for video-conferences and e-learning software failed to materialise despite major technological advances.

Only rarely do large, established companies catch sight of changing needs in the wake of unexpected events, whereas alert entrepreneurs do. The explosive, surprising breakthrough of the Internet, only anticipated by very few, created an entrepreneurial movement unprecedented in world history. Radically new problems and needs arose, for instance, for interface software, browsers, search engines and metacrawlers, email programmes, portals not to mention applications like games, online banking, and so on. Companies like Netscape, Google, Yahoo, Cisco and Lucent Technologies rapidly mushroomed in this fertile entrepreneurial climate.

Conversely, the intense building and construction activities on the Mediterranean Strip in Southern France and Spain are immediate results of an *anticipated* predictable demographic and economic development characterised by a massive migration of people from the north to the south of Europe. A phenomenon that share many characteristics with the influx of people for the northern states of the US to Florida a generation before: more elderly people, more hale elderly people, lower retirement ages, higher pension incomes and assets, an active life style. This friendly entrepreneurial environment has, of course, attracted entrepreneurs and led to the establishment of businesses in many different sectors. Creative market insight in connection with such anticipated well known events can take on the form of flair for optimal timing or situational organisation of a venture including an understanding of factors that create growth.

In any situation, creative market insight has to do with seeing the market in new, unconventional ways, breaking with received wisdom. Sometimes creative market insight can be the outcome of a conscious search for *overlooked events*. The event itself might be well known and exhaustively described as a phenomenon of change and is, in a way, old news, but the event might have been erroneously interpreted and may, therefore, be overlooked or marginalised by the established players. There are many reasons for this – from cannibalisation, oversensitivity to value, loss of competencies of ingrained technologies and an overestimation of the barriers to entry, all the way to confidence in being able to (re)take the market from newcomers in step with the market possibly becoming bigger and more mature.

Golden Valley

On the one hand, the swift dissemination of microwave ovens among private households created expectations of a market for new ready-prepared dishes, packaging and ways of preparing food that could be capitalised by the food industry. Occurrences also prepared the ground for an entirely new product category, viz., the pop-up popcorn which, in record time, became one of the most popular uses for the household microwave oven.

It was not the established snack industry that took the lead in the popcorn race, but a newcomer, Golden Valley, of Minneapolis in Minnesota. Golden Valley was even listed on the New York Stock Exchange before it was acquired by Con Agra.

It is precisely the combination of occurrence and the way information is processed and interpreted by the established companies vis-à-vis the way this is done by entrepreneurs that will determine whether a seed is laid for a future enterprise. Nevertheless, seemingly good news may turn out to be extremely bad for entrepreneurs despite appearance to the contrary:

Amazon.com – and the lemming effect

The news of Amazon.com's – the world's first and biggest Internet shop – total triumph in the book market spread like commercial wildfire all over the world and, in a beautiful combination with undreamt-of access to venture capital, led to a massive influx of new business ventures in the field of Internet-based commerce. However, virtually all companies in the old economy sat on their hands and, accordingly – or so many people thought at the time – lost their only chance of keeping up with the financial gazelles of the new economy. But the news of dot.com stores' unending advantages and unending number of customers in an unending number of product markets was unreliable and wildly exaggerated. The news that the old economy was soon to die and that existing value chains were about to collapse altogether was too good to be true. Actually, entrepreneurs and venture capital made two mistakes. They equated a technical possibility with a business opportunity. They did not analyse the new occurrence critically and in depth. The second mistake was that the lemming effect took over. It led to adverse selection in which venture capitalists invested in internet businesses just because others did. The bubble was a reality.

How is it possible in a systematic way to trace and understand occurrences indicating the anticipated arrival of new markets? And the time when this is going to take place?

The answer is far from simple, but has to do with understanding if and to what extent customers' perceived problems (needs) will *change* as a result of the occurrence. As long as we are speaking of unexpected occurrences, it goes without saying that the problem analysis can only start after the occurrence of the event. Once something has happened. Perhaps a chain reaction.

Kanitech and Free Pen

Gradually more people are suffering from more serious mouse injuries. This development has certainly not come as a surprise, but is a logical consequence of the fast dissemination and growing use of computers. Traditional mouse concepts have gradually become ever more ergonomically correct – but without anybody actually being able to solve the mouse injury problem. The supposition would have to be that what was needed was an efficient, ergonomic solution to the growing number of RSI cases caused by the computer mouse. A different concept.

The vision formulated by the company Kanitech was to develop an entirely new type of mouse – or rather, non-mouse, which in one fell swoop would solve the serious problem that mouse injury had gradually become. Free Pen, as the project was named, takes the form of a pen, and is used in the same way as a pen.

The user pushes the pen across a mat, and in this way moves the cursor on the computer screen. A slight pressure by the pen corresponds to a mouse click. An ordinary user can become entirely familiar with the Free Pen in less than an hour; it is, incidentally, easy to install. Free Pen is cordless and will work as far away as five meters from the computer, for which reason the user is liberated from a monotonous work posture.

When Free Pen was first introduced at the most important European IT trade fair, interest was huge and reviews glowing. Fairly soon Kanitech had distributors in a number of countries, and orders began pouring in. At the same time, Kanitech began developing the second generation of Free Pen with a fancier, more aerodynamic design than that of the first, basic model.

Several scientific articles were published on this new solution. But Free Pen was never a hit with the users. It remained uncontested that the problem of mouse injury had become considerable, and that the conventional solutions were still incapable of remedying the problem.

During the same period, a small firm, IMS, developed the e-learning programme Ergo Saver, sponsored by a big insurance company. This programme, which gives the user advice about working postures and prevention of injury, was a major hit and was successfully exported to a number of countries.

Kanitech saw the new occurrence, recognised the problem and wondered why the established industry had not addressed it efficiently. In many ways, the Free Pen solution was brilliant and cool. Nevertheless the project failed. What went wrong for Kanitech and Free Pen? Perhaps the cause should be looked for among the critical success factors such as users' selection criteria and insufficient distribution power.

And it was Nokia

Why was it Nokia and not Ericsson or Motorola which came to dominate the global market for mobile phones? The "upstart" Nokia simply captured and interpreted the faint noises from the market earlier and better than the others, and today seems to have delivered irrefutable proof of entrepreneurial excellence.

Both Motorola and Ericsson are among the world's strongest when it comes to technical development and functional design. Their unique competencies have yielded leading positions in many different markets in IT and telecommunication. But at one point in time, it was not really so much a matter of technology, engineering focus and technical quality. It was more a matter of listening to the market and reading the signals of change that it was emitting. As far as Motorola was concerned, the company reached the dead end of its technical blind alley only in 1998 when, within the framework of a joint venture, they took part in launching the Iridium, the first purely satellite based telephone, which could do everything (it did not work indoors, though), weighed one kilo and cost $3000. Nokia caught sight of the fact that brand new, gigantic customer segments – geographically and demographically – were about to emerge. It was price, branding, comfort, simplicity and software that were becoming decisive selection criteria – rather than durability and technical sophistication. The fact that it got excellent cooperation from suppliers, together with giving priority to distribution, enabled Nokia to outmanoeuvre the former market leader by grasping approximately 40% of a swiftly growing world market.

Curiosity and novelty gave Nokia a crystal clear insight into the problem. Nokia realised that seen through the eyes of the customer, more is not necessarily better.

Throughout its history, the company, founded in 1865, had produced everything from toilet paper to rubber boots, tires to cables and TV-sets. Finally, the innovative Nokia culture found the needle in the haystack.

Complementarity is a special class of occurrence which, at one and the same time, opens up and closes down new entrepreneurship, often on the basis of various industry-related universes such as cars and petrol stations, railway tracks and trains. The question that an entrepreneur may ask himself is, "Has anything happened in market x for which it is possible to create a symbiosis or interdependence?" Joe Mansueto and Morningstar is a clear example of such a derived business opportunity.

Joe Mansueto and Morningstar

Investment funds constitute the best opportunity for small investors to invest on the stock market. In the early 1980s, the investment fund industry in the USA grew fairly rapidly. There was no reliable information available concerning the funds and their yields, or it was not available to the man in the street. So the private investor did not have the necessary tools to identify, analyse and compare investment funds. This state of affairs actually put a break on the continuing development of the idea behind investment funds.

Joe Mansueto, a young, promising, professional economist, believed that this kind of information should be freely available to everybody. He decided that he would try to structure and democratise valid information on investment funds, and established the company Morningstar. The first edition of Morningstar's "The Sourcebook", published in 1984 and quite affordable for private investors, became a success and soon had benchmark status when it came to benefiting investors as well as fund suppliers and managers. Later on, Morningstar set the world standard as the leading, independent brand in rating investment funds. From the outset, the company and investment funds have developed successfully as each other's companions, and the Internet provided the Morningstar concept and star ratings with strong penetration.

In the case of Morningstar, interdependence is manifest, although, the investment industry would probably have existed in any case, even without ratings and free information for all.

Changes in one market can, if they are interpreted thoughtfully and with due diligence, lead to insights into problems that will allow *substitution* solutions in an entirely different market.

For a long time, the company Dupont, which discovered the material nylon, had been focusing on parachutes. When this market crumbled after World War II leaving Dupont with a sales problem, and when women's liberation in the USA became more widespread, a perfect substitution opportunity appeared, as nylon was excellently suited to make thin, affordable stockings for a mass market that could not afford silk.

Substitution may look quite coincidental: the insulation material rock-wool that turned out to have excellent properties as pot mould in horticultural enterprises – a discovery which the Rockwool Company exploited in a very efficient manner. Hydrocolloid bandages, originally intended for ostomy patients, but which Coloplast managed to develop into the sports product Compeed; before the development of Compeed there was no quick and safe treatment of blisters and pressure sores without any discomfort.

It is never a simple matter to find your bearings for where and when a certain new occurrence holds a potential for entrepreneurship. The art lies in the way in which information is processed and combined to provide a lead based on insight.

2.4 Incongruities as a source of ideas

The entrepreneur who is looking for information should not be satisfied with searching for occurrences in his or her endeavours to couple a problem to a business opportunity. Problems are not necessarily new, but equally as often they are latent. They take the form of ingrained habits, inappropriate constants and received wisdom. Incongruities are found in all industries; they are just waiting to be discovered and remedied. But how to catch sight of them? And what is the reason why nobody has been able to remedy them before? The problem is not the incongruity itself, but the fact that it exists and has not been remedied. Let us discuss the concept of incongruity on the basis of some very recent innovative business ventures.

Carlos and Zensys

Carlos Christensen was a successful, young McKinsey consultant who, in 2000, decided to go into business for himself. Carlos was looking for a top-notch idea. Late one night, when he was the only one left up and was ambling around switching off all the lights in his house, it came to him: how very unpractical that you have to operate each and every switch, every lock, every television set, every household appliance by means of switches located all over the house. It takes time, and is inconvenient, energy consuming and, in a way, it feels unsafe. Why doesn't every home have a cordless device in the form of a handheld, programmable, remote control combined with a transmitter/receiver plugged into the socket? Pleasantly dimmed light all over the house by pushing a button. A message that the bulb in the bathroom has gone. Switching on the lights on the ground floor as you approach the house late at night. Soon Carlos found out that the giants of the industry, like Siemens, GE, Westinghouse, Philips had nothing yet on the market. The few systems that already existed on the market were expensive and unwieldy. On that basis and together with two friends he established the Zensys Company.

Over the next few years, Zensys developed an overall technical platform: a robust, wireless protocol, a chip design, etc. Zensys did not see it as belonging to its role to create the end-user product, but instead targeted its efforts at OEM (Original Equipment Manufacturers). Despite the fact that the technical solution that Zensys developed is smart and innovative, it is not the raison d'être of the project. Instead Zensys did something radical about the suspected latent incongruity between the intelligent and the unintelligent home. Zensys closed a gap between a perceived problem and an existing technical possibility. Zensys itself would, furthermore, draw attention to managerial and financial implementing power as one of the hallmarks of the project.

Urban

An ever decreasing number of people read a newspaper every day, and they spend ever less time doing so. In the region of 35% of all young people never even start reading a daily newspaper: their need for news is covered by television, the Internet and radio. Meanwhile, the core readership of the broadsheet papers at the other end of the age spectrum, are dying. Consequently, for years, newspaper publishers in the USA and most of Europe have endeavoured to do something about the decline in circulation figures. One of the results of this development has been the demise of many newspapers, destructive price wars, absurd pricing models to recruit new readers and subscribers, over-focusing on advertising and markets, package deals and distorting cartel formation.

Gradually, the big newspapers – also in Denmark – resigned themselves to believing that constant decline was a given, and that the way ahead would be to diversify into television and electronic media on the basis of a follow-your-customer philosophy. The newspaper publishing houses did not in any way see the manifest incongruity which had gradually arisen between what they offered the market and the market's actual newspaper needs. It took a new entrant to open the eyes of the newspaper publishing houses.

When the Swedish owned media enterprise, MTG, threw the Metro Express onto the market in Copenhagen, the industry seemed unprepared. The Metro Express is a free-of-charge tabloid newspaper financed by advertising; it has now been introduced in many European cities. The paper is distributed in the centres of metropolises such as railway and metro stations, big shopping streets, and shopping centres.

When the Metro Express was launched, The Berlingske Officin (Orkla Media) had to get cracking, and shortly after it launched the Urban as a counter-move against MTG and to be able to defend its lucrative advertising market. All this is trivial. The bombshell was the fact that in record time two free-of-charge papers achieved astronomical readerships and became the most widely read newspapers in the country; suddenly they had become an integral, indispensable part of Copenhagen-in-the-morning. The most interesting thing is that the need for a daily newspaper among the lost customer segments only had to be met in an efficient manner. This was done when a light-weight newspaper hit the streets. The incongruity between the suppositions about the market and the realities about the market was truly a hefty one.

It can be very difficult to catch sight of incongruities, if you are immersed in them on a daily basis. Gradually you cannot see them anymore; they are considered the natural state of affairs. James, the butler in the film about Miss Sophie's 90th birthday, keeps hammering his foot into the head of the tiger skin on the floor, until, under the influence of alcohol, he breaks with his old habit.

It is exactly the great chance for an entrepreneur that the players in mature industries acquire blind spots and repress their knowledge of incongruities which should be followed up. This applies to,

- the erroneous perception of an industry of itself vis-à-vis the reality (blind spots)
- hidden customer segments
- micro segments and narrow niches
- what the industry supplies vis-à-vis customer expectations
- ties and exit barriers

Michael Dell, of Dell Computers, challenged the idea prevalent in the computer industry that computers must be a shelf product. Subsequently, as it turned out, the established computer industry had an "erroneous" perception of itself vis-à-vis the opportunities of the market.

Hidden customer segments are present and potential customer groups which the industry itself has not caught sight of as a segment and whose needs are, therefore, not being met or covered by second-best solutions in comparison to the preferences of the segment. Hidden customer segments form a latent opportunity because, over time, a gap arises between customers' actual needs and the perceived benefits of products. This, among other things, became a trap to daily newspapers.

As the market grows and matures, *micro segments* and narrow niches crystallise. Too small and bothersome for the market leaders, but big enough for entrepreneurial ventures. CBB, for example, is a small business in the field of mobile telephony; the company targets its activities at teenagers. CBB enables its customers to buy and prepay mobile speaking time over the internet, something which is appealing to many in comparison to the post-paid standard packages offered by many big operators.

Sometimes you come across a fundamental incongruity between what an entire industry has to "offer" and customer expectations. With irrepressible strength, the discount supermarket chains squeezed into grocery markets all over the world, because the established chains disregarded a strong wish on the part of the customers for affordable staples and branded goods.

Disappointed expectations cannot exclusively be blamed on deficient insight on the part of the industry into its own market. Cannibalisation together with the structures of the production apparatus and the *ties* this entails, also play a central role. Nowadays, the market for air travel is having a similar experience: low-cost-carriers such as South West Airlines, Go, Ryan, Virgin, and Easy Jet have conquered in record time considerable market shares and brought an old, previously financially strong industry to its knees. The big established airlines have not been capable of changing their ground, tied as they were to high fixed costs, price inelastic business customers, unsound competitive methods, government involvement and high exit barriers.

Incongruities should not tempt anyone to entertain idyllic notions. As a rule, there are good reasons *why* incongruities exist. It is rare for competitors to be completely stupid, and on closer inspection, many problems turn out to be fake opportunities.

2.5 Innovation as a problem detector

When, all of a sudden, it becomes possible to do something nobody has done before, doors are opened for new ventures. Needs and problems present themselves. Consequently, innovation has an obvious chance to offer to the insightful, creative entrepreneur. Here we are not thinking of innovation carried out by the entrepreneur herself, but very much of innovation elsewhere.

When an entrepreneur commercialises an innovation in a different market or in a different context from the one in which the innovation took place, we speak of *transferring*. Transferring is the process in which the entrepreneur moves the innovation from its place of birth to the market, be it geographically, sectorally or in terms of application. Transferring innovation is of crucial importance to economic growth in the investment regime which is on its way to replacing the post-industrial epoch that came to an end around 2000. As an entrepreneur you are no longer tied to the innovations of the areas adjacent to you. Increasingly network technology is overcoming temporal, geographical as well as hierarchical barriers faster than before. Proximity does play a role, but it is no longer quite as crucial.

Innovation as a source of creative market insight is quite tricky and can lead to fatal, faulty conclusions. This will be the case if you allow yourself to think in an uncritical *deductive* manner, epitomised by the following question, "I have come across an epoch making innovation – I wonder where it can be used to start up a new venture?" As we all know, love is blind. The same thing can be said of systematic *induction*: "I have discovered a problem in the market. I wonder whether there is an innovation to cure it."

Your best chance of factoring in innovation into the in-depth understanding of the problem are those situations where either customer problems or innovation is tacit knowledge on the part of the entrepreneur, and where the idea only assumes concrete form when the trails cross. Systematically or randomly.

Some technical innovations turn out to be so revolutionising and potent in value that they set off an avalanche of application. And sometimes it is possible to carry out a systematic search for a set of market problems that can be addressed by retrieving such innovations. Only when Marc Andresen launched the world's first browser in 1994 did the Internet really get its breakthrough, although it had existed for more than 20 years. The tens and thousands of entrepreneurs all over the world who immediately had a feeling for the unending fertility of the Internet and went ahead with developing products targeted at specific sets of problems, got a real boost shortly after. Whereas there was a hundred years between the invention of the steam engine and the world's first railway, there was only 20 years between the birth of the Internet the introduction of the browser and the authentic ketchup effect.

There is no substitute for the originality capable of merging customer need and innovation into an idea. This combinative effect is in itself the life nerve of the innovative prowess of the entrepreneur. However, the innovation track as the path to market insight is not about extrapolating engineering thought into market empathy.

Genius – Ejgil did the right thing

Once upon a time Ejgil Møllsgaard attended a symposium about the application of laser treatment in dental surgery – more specifically periodontal disease. The traditional treatment of acute periodontal disease is surgical and rather traumatic for the patient. Laser treatment, which is non-traumatic and far less painful, seemed the obvious paradigm shift for dental surgery.

Nevertheless, it struck Ejgil that the laser equipment he saw was far from efficient for soft-tissue surgery (periodontal disease) because of the heat development and the consequent unnecessary injury to healthy tissue. Everything seemed to indicate that an entirely new type of laser was needed if laser treatment was to become efficient, safe and without undesirable side effects in connection with periodontal disease. A problem which a lot of adults suffer from without receiving any treatment.

Ejgil developed Genius a so-called Nd Yag-laser endowed with the very properties that would allow painless and effective treatment of periodontal disease. Soon, the product was a hit among young dentists who wished to move forward in new directions.

2.6 Missing links

Missing links are obvious shortcomings, weak links, and the like, whose existence is known to us all, and to which we have all grown accustomed. Here, the problem is neither a new factor nor an incongruity or that something has been overlooked. The need is glaringly obvious, and once the solution has been found, it will be internalised without the least little bit of inertia. This situation calls for entrepreneurship.

Slurry

Slurry is a big problem in modern, intensive, animal husbandry in Western Europe. The farmer stores the slurry in huge tanks and spreads it over his fields to fertilise them. If it becomes possible to develop a separation process and so get water, mineral, dry matter, etc., it will mean that costly storing and spreading of slurry would disappear altogether. Potentially, this missing link represents a very high financial value, and for a long time a small handful of technologies and methods has competed about supplying the proof.

We do not know whether a method will crop up which proves to be so technologically and financially superior that it will become the benchmark. Or whether a number of competing concepts, each with a mix of strengths and weaknesses, will end up sharing the market.

Missing links do not only exist in combined production like farming, but everywhere. In the fields of IT and telecommunication, proprietary solutions lead to insufficient interoperability which, in the final analysis, puts a brake on market development. To remedy or provide substitution for missing links, the most important suppliers have from time to time agreed on a certain industrial standard – Blue Tooth, Web Services, GSM. In other cases, a business venture has managed to grasp the position of being the de facto standard – Microsoft and Windows. By going for the missing links, the entrepreneur takes on at least one of two challenges, and frequently both:

- A product development race with other ventures working with the same set of problems.
- A receptivity and marketing race with competing solutions and dominant perceptions.

2.7 Inventory: creative market insight

The mental journey from the first impulse and spontaneous idea to an in-depth understanding of a need is challenging, full of deep chasms and high peaks that are more than difficult to traverse.

Below is a checklist for processing market problems. It has been designed as a series of confrontational contentions everybody can process in order to get under the skin of the specific problem in the market in which a business opportunity is thought to be embedded.

The checklist has been constructed on the basis of the themes, deliberations and principles described in this chapter with the addition of a few new aspects.

The guide should not be seen as a list for which there are true and false answers. It should be seen as a source of inspiration identifying and highlighting problems and for testing opportunities. You should accept the word "problem" instead of the more commonly used "need". 3M, so well known for its market innovative management in such disparate fields as tapes for use in households and offices, medical products, safety, packaging, connectors for the electronics industry, to name a few, has a very precise way of expressing creative market insight, "We solve unsolved problems"!

		CONTENTION	OPINION/COMMENT
I		*My original approach*	
	A	I have located a problem in the market	
	B	I have had a bright idea which I think could be an opportunity	
	C	I have a product on the drawing board based on my own knowledge	
	D	I have special insight into the market	
	E	I have identified a market where I believe a problem can be tracked down	
II		*I think something has occurred in the market which will yield an opening because*	
	A	The needs of some customers are changing, which the industry has overlooked or chosen to disregard	
	B	The selection criteria of the customers are shifting, but very few people have observed this yet	
	C	The market is expanding quickly, and there is always room for one more supplier	
	D	Entirely new customer segments or scopes of application are emerging, but the industry has not caught sight of them	
	E	My competitors are busy waging war against each other, and do not expect any new entrants	

F	Something entirely unexpected has occurred, which can be exploited if I react quickly	
G	Something is happening outside the market, which I believe can generate an opportunity, and which only few people have observed	
H	There is no market today, but I think one will arise, because customer perception is that they have a problem	
III	**I have observed incongruities in the market**	
A	The industry's perception of itself is not in accordance with realities – there are blind spots	
B	Hidden market segments exist	
C	The solutions offered to the customers simply are not good enough/too costly	
D	Niches exist which the big players cannot be bothered to do anything about	
E	The industry is hidebound and does not live up to consumer expectations	
F	The industry is frozen and the needs of large customer segments are not met	
IV	**The market opening is caused by an innovation to which the established industry does not seem to react**	
A	New knowledge makes it possible to solve a hitherto unsolved problem, and not many in the industry have seen this	
B	New knowledge makes it possible to solve a problem in a better or completely different way	
C	New knowledge makes it possible to solve a problem in a less costly way	
D	The innovation aims at solving entirely new needs	
E	It is my specific innovation (technology/product idea) which makes this possible	
F	I am among the very few people who have caught sight of the innovation's m application	

G	I have discovered an entirely new market	
V	***I think I have discovered the answer to the missing link***	
A	I have discovered how the weakest link in a process can be strengthened or remedied	
B	I believe that a redesign of the process can solve a serious problem	
C	I know how to complete the process	
D	I have discovered exactly what the customer is missing	
VI	***Why has nobody solved the problem efficiently before?***	
A	No supplier has discovered that there is a problem here	
B	Customers did not know that they had a problem	
C	Customers' switching costs are high, but will drop quickly	
D	The problem has been solved, but not in a good or affordable way	
E	Until now, the problem has not been serious enough	
F	Something new will always be associated with uncertainty	
G	People have become accustomed to this state of affairs and do not think it can be changed	
VII	***What is my greatest uncertainty concerning the problem in which I think a market opportunity is embedded?***	
A	The problem is not understood well enough from the point of view of customers: do they perceive a problem, and if yes, why?	

B	The problem is only relevant as a business idea if many customers want a solution	
C	A crucial detail is overlooked	
D	The problem is not urgent enough for the customers	
E	The problem solving itself	
F	The problem is solved in a completely different way than I imagine today	
G	Somebody else almost found another solution	
H	Too tied to a specific solution – product, technology, etc.	

Assessment of a market problem

The purpose of the inventory is to assist the early phase of analysis and take up points for discussion, which an entrepreneur might easily overlook or underestimate. This inventory does not invite quantitative grading, but dialogue, self-criticism, and examination of needs; in this way, it is hoped, it will be possible to map out a route to creative market insight.

Accordingly, Servolink is the story of the brilliant solution which ran into a wall of resistance which might possibly have been revealed in advance by creative market insight.

The Servolink story 1984

It was, and still is, a major problem that wheelchair users found it difficult to serve themselves at petrol stations, banks and gain access to buildings.

Servolink was a transmission-reception system for which a transmitter installed in the disabled person's car or wheelchair could activate a receiver inside the building and, in this manner, ensure natural and dignified personal service. The company Servolink designed a characteristic, easily recognisable logo that was mounted in a place which the disabled person could see, and so was in a position to assess whether the location in question was equipped with the system, and therefore accessible.

With the introduction of Servolink, wheelchair users achieved far better freedom of movement, and a brilliant future was prophesied for the product. Servolink had no competitors, and the financial decision makers in most local authorities were willing to cover the acquisitioning costs for the wheelchair users. The major petrol companies, banks, etc., were positive; they bought the idea and installed the Servolink system in the retail part of the chain.

No doubt, Servolink solved a serious, genuine problem for individuals, and there was no serious resistance from those industries who had to pay for it. Nevertheless, Servolink never had the success that the project deserved. It flopped. As it turned out, the organisations for the disabled were opposed. The reason for their opposition was that Servolink was only the second-best solution. The first-best solution would be for all buildings to be modified to allow a wheelchair user the same kind of access as everybody else. The organisations appealed to their members to boycott Servolink, and this appeal was followed by enough people to prevent the system from ever really catching on.

The conclusion to be drawn is that market orientation plays a crucial role for good entrepreneurship. Entrepreneurship in a market orientated perspective can be seen as a competency in which planning and execution form a synthesis. Even ventures based on technically superior innovations will be well advised to ensure an understanding of perceived problems, far beyond the knowledge possessed by existing companies in a particular field. What is business acumen other than a sublime understanding of customers and a superior sense of timing?

Literature

Ardichivili Alexander, Lardozo Richard, Ray Sourav: *A Theory of Entrepreneurial Opportunity Identification and Development.* Journal of Business Venturing. 2000.

Drucker Peter F.: *Innovation and Entrepreneurship – practice and principles.* Butterworth, London. 1986 (1999).

Drucker Peter F.: *The Discipline of Innovation.* Harvard Business Review, Nov-Dec 1998 s 149 – 156.

Duus Henrik Johannsen: *Economic Foundation for an Entrepreneurial Marketing Concept.* Scandinavian Journal of marketing. 1997.

EVCA: *The Global Competitiveness Report.* 2002.

FORA (Økonomi- og Erhvervsministeriet): *Et benchmark studie af iværksætter-aktivitet – hvad kan Danmark lære.* 2002.

Franklin Carl: *Why innovations fail*. Spiro Press. London. 2003.

Guiltinan J og Paul G: *Marketing Management: Strategies and Programmes*. Mc.Graw Hill. 1991.

Harper David A.: *Entrepreneurship and the market process*. Rothledge. London. 1996.

Henry Jane, Walker David (ed): *Managing Innovation*. Sage Publications. London. 1991.

Hougaard Søren: *Den Markedsorienterede Virksomhed*. Working Paper. Copenhagen Business School. 1994.

Pearson Alan W. Ed. By Henry Jane, Walker David*: Managing Innovation: An Uncertainty Reduction process.* Sage Publications. London. UK. 1991.

3. The window of opportunity[20]

"When the wind of changes blow, some build
wind protection, others build windmills."

Mao Tse-tung

Creative market insight opens a passage to the *window of opportunity*, the subject of the present chapter. An opportunity can be described as the chance for the entrepreneur to meet market needs through a creative combination of resources, whereby exceptional value is generated.[21] The path to a business idea goes through the window of opportunity.

A business opportunity may arise when, for a moment, the window of opportunity is left open or at least ajar – and also if the knowledgeable and audacious business person manages to prise open the closed window.

The thesis behind the expression "window of opportunity": business opportunities are not just lying there – they are created by means of alertness, creativity, networks and systematic methodology.[22]

This chapter introduces and discusses various types of windows and opportunity domains. It surveys the *grid of opportunities* through a systematic identification of fields containing the chance of creating extraordinary value. Furthermore, the window of opportunity is illustrated in relation to the entrepreneur's competency profile and approaches to the market.

The crucial mental transition from insight into the opportunity to determine the *congregation* constitutes the first, and perhaps the most serious real test of strength – the showdown – between the business idea and the market.

This chapter also stamps out some of the dogmatic ideas concerning the window of opportunity – here represented by the paradoxes of the chance creating factors.

---

20 Derek Abell (1979, 1980) speaks of strategic windows.
21 Schumpeter (1934), Kirzner (1973) according to Hills (1994)
22 Henry and Walker (1991)

3.1 The window of opportunity, entrepreneurship and luck

When embarking upon identifying a business idea, it is important to keep need and opportunity separate in the thinking process. The presence of existing or future needs does not necessarily mean that a business opportunity is within reach. The identification of unmet needs is a necessary – but not a sufficient – condition for success.

Chicago

Just like clothes make the man, we might be equally justified in asserting that opportunities make the needs. More than any other, the entertainment industry focuses on opportunity. In the movie Chicago, the singers Roxy and Velma, who have both been acquitted of a murder which each of them has, in fact, committed, try to get a solo career going as a cabaret singer in the nightclubs of the city. However, they are both turned down time and time again by nightclub proprietors: a jazz murderess has not got any pull. By way of a last resort, they decide to cooperate by singing together as the two jazz murderesses instead of competing, and the authentic ketchup effect is the result. People go mad to see two murderesses together on stage. It is Velma who catches sight of the business opportunity and who sells Roxy on the idea: "People have seen one jazz murderess entertain before, but two ....". The window of opportunity was closed for the conventional solution, but was open to the creative combination of resources.

Students like to take up the discussion of needs versus opportunities. Normally they are of the sensible opinion that needs (demand) are very often governed by the possibilities (supply), not the other way around. The argument that most of the things with which we surround ourselves in working and private life are there only because someone invented them without first making sure that the need – the perceived deficit – existed, seems sustainable enough. People, as it were, do not know what they need before they can buy it. The evidence is overwhelming.

This discussion is always annoyingly unproductive; it divides the participants into two camps and is never settled by any convincing explanation or approximation to an agreement. It peters out and leaves everybody confused and unclear. Theoretical sophistries concerning generic versus specific needs do not tend to reduce the confusion.[23]

Unless a venture originates in an artistic urge or sudden whim, the distinction between problem (need) and possibility – between diagnosis and remedy – is quite central, irrespective of the direction of the cause-effect connection because,

- It maintains an unambiguous focus on customers: does the need exist? Now?
- It makes the competency requirements facing the venture visible: are we skilful enough? Do we know enough? Have we got the guts?
- It calls for a combination of the elements: Have we got a chance of meeting a market need and create exceptional value by means of a creative new combination of resources?

As a result, the three factors: need, competency and exceptional value, will determine whether the window of opportunity is open or will be capable of being opened. It will always be a matter of taking a chance in which unknown quantities are at play, for which reason risks will be considerable. Life, after all, is a game of chance – also for the enterprising individual.

Even big, experienced, highly professional companies, who understand their markets with all their nooks and crannies, will launch a high percentage of new products that fail, despite the fact that, apparently, everything has been examined and tested in advance. Misinterpreting the window of opportunity is not the privilege of the entrepreneur.

The sound of Gallaway

Gallaway, one of the world's leading manufacturers of golfing equipment introduced a newly developed club, a super-driver, targeted particularly at the US market. The driver was superior to all previous models and designs as far as performance was concerned, i.e. length and reliability of the stroke. Expectations ran high.

---

23 The concept of opportunity: "An opportunity can be defined as a desirable future stage that is different from the current stage and that is deemed feasible to achieve…..
Therefore opportunity is about feasible change – a favourable direction to reach a future stage…". Hills et. Alt. (1994)

However, not long after, Gallaway had to conclude that the driver was not a hit in the USA, and the early series were sold at high discounts in Europe. What was wrong with the product? It did not sound right. The tiny "click" of a driver hitting the ball in the sweat-spot is a beautiful sound to the golf player and an inseparable part of the joys of the game. In this case, the click-sound of the driver had a pitch which was slightly too low and base-like, almost a "clack". That was enough to motivate a rejection by the pernickety US consumer: insufficient satisfaction of the need for a particular sound. A failing mark in phonetics. What was apparently an inferior criterion for selection became the critical factor.

The key to the market – the window of opportunity – is located where competency encounters a new or existing need, and where exceptional value is, therefore, generated, however, always with the proviso that no unforeseeable details interfere or bad luck occurs. The situation is illustrated in the figure below:

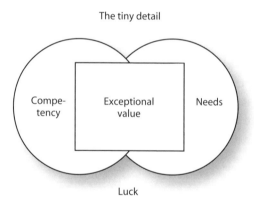

Figure 3.1 The window of opportunity – a simple, mental model

It might seem unprofessional to use a concept like luck in connection with entrepreneurship. Better planning, more careful risk analysis, deeper simulation of the business logic, using more advanced forecasting techniques, etc., surely will enable replacing intuition and serendipity with rationality and solid calculations? The answer is no. In practice, we cannot draw the conclusion that the most careful entrepreneur, by definition, is also the luckiest one; that with due diligence things will work out – it is up to you as an entrepreneur to search out your own luck. We all know that the Emperor Napoleon I distinguished between lucky and gifted generals, and he definitely preferred the former category. Franklin's (2003) study of the factors that lead to success and failure, respectively, for new enterprises, substantiates this assertion by drawing the conclusion that the clear number one among all the success factors examined is being able to "take advantage of random events". This factor leads to 13 times as many successes as failures.

An analogy of good luck in the field of advanced technology speaks of *periods of opportunities* versus *periods of excitement* (cif. Chapter 8). For a few moments or periods, a technology has an exceptional value. If such a propitious moment is missed what we get is a lengthier period, during which the technology is to be refined, versionised, developed, applied, etc., but has no market value. Excitement, in this connection, is ironical.

3.2 A business venture typology

The successful combination of competencies and needs (= creative market insight) can be crystallised into four different types of business venture, each based on its own assumption of the window of opportunity and its structure. The four types can be illustrated in the following simplified manner:

		Perceptual window: Opportunity engendered by creative market insight – customer need	
		Undefined need	Well defined need
Conceptual window: Opportunity created by the value generating competency	Undefined competency	Dream	Problem solution
	Well defined competency	Technology transfer	Enterprise formation

Table 3.1 Different types of ventures as gateways to the market

Source: Inspiration from Ardichivili, Lardozo, Ray (2000)

Ventures that have their origin in competencies or unexploited resources represent a different approach than that which uses problems and needs as their points of departure. At the same time the two approaches reflect the theoretical distinction between the inside-out resource based view of competitive advantages versus the outside-in perspective (structure-conduct-performance) – cif. Chapter 1.

Dreams of the window of opportunity, the situation in which both needs and competencies are unclear, may assume different forms. The extremely visionary entrepreneur will, for instance, set up the following equation: If it was possible to …., it would be extremely exciting to …., or imagine that it ever became possible to ….. Not infrequently do the dreams and searches of charismatic and forward-looking people of the untrodden paths lead to the opening of entirely new possibilities. Utopian ideas, imagination and innovation are not far removed from one another. The ability to think completely unconventionally sometimes leads to surprising results that will generate value – but this was not so in the Catenas case.

Catenas – a dream of strategy and communications consultancy

The answer to the question of who it was that really had the idea of what was later to become the worldwide consultancy network Catenas is lost in the impenetrable mists of history. However, there is no doubt that the listed venture capital company 2M Invest had great faith in the idea and invested nearly 60 million Euro in the project before it crashed. The theory behind Catenas (the Roman name for a beautiful antique arc) was the following: At the time, web bureaus and e-consultancy firms with their exorbitant stock-market values – but also with very narrow and frail competencies – were at their height. During the same period the biggest consultancy firms changed their focus. De facto, they assigned a lower priority to classic strategic consulting in favour of implementing IT-system.

The idea behind Catenas was to collect some of the best and most focused strategy and communications enterprises in the world into one single group so that customers – the big corporations – could benefit from one-stop shopping. And, mind you, not one-stop shopping among consultancy mastodons, but among the best niche-players globally speaking. Catenas was to develop into a global supermarket uniting state-of-the-art competencies into one single service concept linked in a network in which it was possible to exploit centralised and decentralised advantages.

The realisation of the vision itself was effected through a series of swift investments in minority share holdings in consultancy firms, web-bureaus and communications firms in the USA and Europe. The model were that Catenas would acquire minority share holdings in these firms which would, at the same time, buy shares in Catenas and subscribe to the Catenas constitution.

Unfortunately, Catenas did not offer the unique kind of growth which the market was looking for, just as the competencies of the venture were unilaterally targeted at swift growth and did, perhaps, underestimate the importance of integration between the business units of the Catenas family. Catenas went bust together with 2M Invest in 2002.

Catenas had a glimpse of the window of opportunity and, potentially, might have created exceptional value, but lost everything in the execution; another reason for this might be that an objective of quick exit through stock market listing reduces preparedness for change.

If you have conceived an idea, but do not have the know-how and experience to prise open the window of opportunity here and now, this will always be a poisonous cocktail. It is the fate of the opportunist to wait for Dame Fortune.

On the other hand, the window of opportunity is standing wide open when the impulse is born in the shape of an innovative *problem solution* of a well defined customer problem. The purely market orientated opportunity will always run into a lot of difficulties in product development and commercialisation, either because the project is short of concrete competency, or because the entrepreneur finds it difficult to understand what is missing or overlooks essential external conditions. However, the problem-solving entrepreneur will focus on the end result and acts in an agile manner, because, at all times, customer needs are at the centre of their attention. Perhaps that was the reason why companies like IBM, Sun, Oracle and Microsoft did, at the end of the day, beat giants like GE, RCA, Philips and Siemens, companies that did at the time have superior resources at their disposal and should, therefore, have been capable of conquering the software market, something for which they did, in fact, fight hard in the early stages of the market. Some of the best known and most admired innovations in history have been based on *technology transfer* – random or planned coupling of unique competencies and an undefined need.

In some situations, uncertainty concerning the use and focus of a certain innovation is a fact, and will therefore require a reversal of logics. The possibility exists prior to the recognition of the need. The possibility creates the need.

"Post it" is a result of Spencer Silver's research at 3M, which led to a highly unexpected outcome – a not very efficient type of glue. The most negative thing you can say about glue is that it does not glue things together, and that was precisely what was true about this glue. So for nearly five years there was no problem to this solution. Naturally enough, the 3M product development department concentrated on developing glue – not a poorer one and gradually the non-glue was forgotten. But not by everyone.

Silver's colleague, Carl Fry, often went to church and was a chorister in the church choir. One day in church he was quite irritated by the fact that his bookmark kept falling out of the hymnbook disturbing his concentration. The thought of Spencer Silver and his peculiar adhesive gel came to him ….. The outcome? Post it …

Identification of new hitherto undiscovered fields of application and need for existing technologies and competencies which the entrepreneur masters may turn out to be a big opportunity. Brian Head proved this when, despite innumerable fiascos and disappointments, he finally had a break-through for his metal skis.

Technology transfer does not in every situation represent an entrepreneurial opportunity. Only if you are creative, knowledgeable and stubborn enough, only if the established companies in an industry (= the competitors) overlook or disregard the threat, and only if the benefits to the customers are significant can the window of opportunity be prised open. Kodak, for example, is still a market leader in the photo field despite radical technical changes in the history of photography – Polaroid, digitalisation, etc., all of which are threats to Kodak. However, Kodak has managed to bar the window of opportunity to all technology transferring entrepreneurial would-be entrants.

The Swiss watch industry constitutes a similar example. Despite the fact that in the early 1970s Japanese watch manufactures caught the Swiss unawares in launching electronic products, something which enabled them quickly to conquer considerable market shares, the Swiss brands have, 30 years later, retaken large shares of the world market. Japanese technology transfer did not lead to incontestable and insurmountable competitive advantages. The Swiss watch industry regained its former market strength by means of product innovation – including the integration of quartz works into plastic houses – and launched Swatch with the support of a massive communications effort.

The below list of positive and negative indicators shows whether and to what extent the possibility of an entrepreneur for successful technology transfer – in addition, of course, to his belief in an indisputable utility for the customer – is realistic.

Green lights – positive signals:	Red lights – negative signals:
• *Reversibility* – customers can test the possibility of "annulling the deal"	• *Considerable acquisition cost* without the chance of prior testing
• *Risk* – the concept is used in relative isolation and is not part of integrated functions or processes	• *The technology is "mission critical"* and must be integrated with other sub-systems and functions or profoundly impact on consumer patterns or the image of the customer
• *Focused application* in which competency and technology determine the competitiveness of the customer	• The technology has *many scopes of application* and is not adapted to a single, specific application
• *Low transaction costs*: contact, contract and control costs are low	• *Process of acquisition is troublesome and costly*

Table 3.2 Technology transfer: red and green lights for entrepreneurs

Even superior and unique technologies may have difficulties in squeezing through the window of opportunity.

HotCache from Nowco

Nowco had developed a unique real-time technology. Real-time cores are used in many different applications in which it is necessary that data and messages reach many users at the exact same nanosecond. Therefore real time is used for instance in the financial sector, in defence, for surveillance, entertainment, and in financial control, all of them fields in which asymmetrical information may generate high costs, flawed quality, errors and risk.

The HotCache technology from Nowco broke away from conceived wisdom according to which all data is transmitted point-to-point from a server – also known as the star-typology. Instead Nowco developed a data-bus so that data could flow in real time multipoint to multipoint without going through a server.

This pioneering bus-technology carries a long series of incontestable advantages for many customer segments. The platform was developed for a specific application in the field of surveillance. However, it turned out to be extremely difficult to transfer the technology to other uses and customers despite the fact that it was superior to the conventional solution as far as quality, efficiency and nominal price were concerned. Where was the window of opportunity – the chance of successful technology transfer? The preconditions for the green lights were not present from the start.

The difficulty for HotCache was the irreversibility of the technology and its high degree of integration compared to the other systems which the customer already had. The technology was perceived as very promising indeed, but at the same time risky to take on board. The perceived real price in acquiring HotCache, thereby leaving behind well-know solutions, turned out to be astronomical.

If the entrepreneur has a well-defined competency which will meet similarly well-defined customer needs, we speak of *enterprise formation*. In this situation the level of uncertainly is distinctly lower than was the case for technology transfer for which the reception barriers of the customer segment are serious, unknown factors. In professional service industries it is a matter of enterprise formation when the engineer or the dentist establishes his or her own practice. The start of Pressalits also is about enterprise formation.

Pressalit improves the esthetical and functional quality of the bathroom

In 1954, three tradesmen started an enterprise on the basis of an idea in which they firmly believed: pressing toilet seats in a new material to replace the wooden and bakelite seats that were in common use at the time. One day, two of the tradesmen, Christian P. Larsen and Holger Christensen, had been working with gluing together some furniture. At the end of the day, they went home without having discovered that the glue pot had fallen over on the radiator and slid down unto the floor where the glue had become mixed with some sawdust. When they discovered the accident a few days later, the mixture had grown into a hard compound. They thought that this might be useful for something, and their supposition was confirmed by a chemical analysis. Glue and fine wooden fibres were pressed and turned out to have excellent properties for toilet seats: hygienic and easy to clean, extremely strong and durable, well suited for mass production.

Today Pressalit produces 1.5 million toilet seats a year in 100 different designs and 150 colour tones.

3.3 Domains of opportunities

Irrespective of whether the seed for entrepreneurship is the state-of-the-art competency, the obvious customer need, the technical possibility, the beautiful vision or the original perspective, alertness, creativity and diagnostic clarity are necessary prerequisites if the window of opportunity is to be opened. Sensing, discovering, creating and evaluating are, therefore, key processes of entrepreneurship. Ultimately, insight into needs as well as into resources constitutes the combinatorics by means of which the outlines of a viable business idea can be drawn up.

In this connection you can make an intersection into the domain of opportunities by asking, "In which context can opportunities arise, and how do they arise?" Table 3.3 illustrates this:

	Special interest	**As part of a job**
Systematic research	Passion	Method
Random discovery	Curiosity	Alertness

Table 3.3 Domains of opportunities

The subdivision indicated of the domains of opportunities has a systematics-randomness "axis", and a distinction between interest-driven opportunities on the one hand and creations made under the auspices of a job on the other.

It may appear artificial to subdivide the domains of opportunities into cells with boundaries, since in nearly all cases it will be a matter of mixes. The element of surprise – the magical moment – cannot be dispensed with or replaced, no matter how method-governed, passion-driven, alert and sequential a development process may be. Without discovery – no discovery.

Sony

In Sony's cassette tape-recorder division they were trying to redesign the small portable tape-recorder which could reproduce sound in stereo. Unfortunately it was not possible to reduce the size enough, and at the end of the day, the engineers were left with a gadget that could not record – it could only play. They used it to listen to while working.

One day, Mr Ibuka, chairman of the board, happened to come by, he saw the gadget and was reminded of a development project in another part of the organisation where they were working to create a light-weight, portable headset. The rest is history – the Walkman was born.

The Sony example does not attempt to paint a romantic picture of business opportunities as a result of mere coincidence. More likely than not, Sony had thousands of projects lying in their drawers and not just this single one that lead to a moment of magical insight. In the situations where the fairy godmother suddenly appears, her magical wand will normally point at the extremely professional and focused entrepreneur. It was hardly by pure coincident that it was Alexander Fleming who discovered penicillin, although it looked like a random discovery. Nor that it was Christian Hansen who caught sight of an odd yeast fungus in a dark and damp staircase; later it turned out to have excellent qualities in the dairy sector.

3.4 The grid of opportunity as a diagnostic method

Some opportunities arise along an *imitative axis* in which the operative words are imitation and "me too". In some market situations there will always be room for one more – typically because the market is growing fast while, at the same time, entry barriers are low. In other cases, the entrepreneurial venture squeezes its way into the market by being marginally better or cheaper, or by targeted copying like the kind we see in the field of pharmaceuticals. Imitation can be a fairly risk-free window of opportunity unless a market leader is being directly attacked and considers itself in serious jeopardy.

Things are different when the entrepreneurial venture is moving along the *innovative axis*, where the heading is renewal. Renewal of technology, processes, material, organisation, habits, fashion, etc., entails more uncertainties and iterations.

In the search for and the description of the window of opportunity the *grid of opportunity* may be a practical diagnostic method, cif. table 3.4:

The six phases in the buyer's cycle of experience						
	Purchase	Delivery	Use	Supplement	Maintenance	Scrapping
Produc- tivity						
Simplifi- cation						
Con- venience						
Risk						
Image, Pleasure						
Environ- mental friend- liness						

(Left axis label: **The six value drivers**)

Table 3.4 Grid of opportunity

Source: Inspiration from Kim and Mauborgne (2000)

The grid of opportunity operates with two dimensions: the *customer lifecycle* and the *value drivers*

The value drivers are not universal, but must be adjusted to the characteristics of the specific area of need.

Using the grid of opportunity forces the entrepreneur to focus on the question of where exactly in the cycle of experience the idea generates extraordinary perceived value, and why. The grid encourages creative, but also systematic market insight, precise clarification of needs and, perhaps most important of all, processing of the question: What decisive new values are embedded in the idea, which – in the perception of the customer – are not provided by the existing solutions in the market?

Analytical formulas may lead to rigidity if they are given in excessive doses or they will clip the wings of creativity unnecessarily. However, they may be excellent sources of inspiration for locating problems – new factors, incongruities, missing links, innovations – and as the very first success indicator during the phase in which the entrepreneur is most in need of validation of his idea.

Ecco Shoes is an excellent example of an enterprise that saw the opportunity to create exceptional value for consumers by targeting the value field of convenience in the use phase.

Let people's feet call the tune

In 1963, when Karl Toosby founded Ecco Shoes it was in real terms a revolutionary idea that shoes ought to fit people's feet – and not the other way around. "Let people's feet call the tune". Today most of us think that this is stating the obvious, and Ecco Shoes are very much associated with comfort, diversity, freedom and timelessness. In 1963, this philosophy was certainly not a mainstream philosophy. At the time, shoes did not fit very well; chiropodists and Dr. Scholl had the time of their lives. Fashion called for stiletto heals for women and pointed shoes for men without any support for the arches. Shoes for everyday use were mass produced without any special attention being paid to people's feet – strange as it may seem. Ecco had its breakthrough in 1978 and for many years after, Ecco was associated with a sensible, natural look in the negative sense: Un-cool, inelegant, certainly practical and durable, but not very compatible with most people's wish to be stylish.

Today Ecco is a brand with a completely different position – not least out in the wide world where no one recalls the early Ecco collections. One of Denmark's most noteworthy business fairytales bears a lot of resemblance to The Ugly Duckling: 9,000 employees, annual sales of 12 million pairs and an annual turnover of more than Euro 450 million distributed over 45 markets. It all began with the grid of opportunity. Shoes that fit. Shoes that are well designed. The vision of the consumer who wants convenience, quality and comfort without having to compromise. Respect for the customer. How difficult can it be?

Retrospectively, you may well wonder why all of the mature and competition-intensive shoe industry of that time did not bustle to be the first and the biggest to climb through the quality window, but left the stage to entrepreneurs like Toosbuy. However, at all times, all industries have their predominant logic and, because of that, unintentionally they leave room for the sublime innovation.

One way in which it is possible to combine imagination and systematics is by asking the following questions:

- How can a single utility factor be exploited in a new phase in the customer's cycle of experience?
- How can a new utility factor create added value in the same phase of the customer's lifecycle?

3.5 Opportunity and lifecycle

The lifecycle represents a special form of generating opportunities. The theoretical rationale behind lifecycle in the form of diffusion of innovations is described in further detail in Chapter 8.

It falls outside the scope of this book to go through the courses that lifecycles can take and what the consequences of these may turn out to be for entrepreneurial ventures. However, a few points attract special interest in relation to the window of opportunity.

Lifecycle is an ex post abstraction, that is to say, a course event that will only be known after it has taken place. Lifecycle does not follow laws like those that are followed by physics or mathematics, they are incalculable.[24] It is the exception rather than the rule that it is possible to forecast a future lifecycle with anything resembling certainty. Innovations, changing customer preferences, substituting solutions and many other things can act as spanners in the works and change a lifecycle suddenly and unpredictably.

The inflection points[25] in the lifecycle cif. figure 3.2 attract a very special interest as these points contain the most spectacular opportunities and threats. The world is not linear and reversible, if it were the entrepreneur would not find many golden eggs.

---

24 It could be claimed that lifecycle is an incontestable law of nature, but that only a microscopic proportion of products actually manages to go through the entire cycle. Thus, the problem is not the lifecycle, but natural selection. And precisely that is the challenge facing the entrepreneur: ensuring that he is among those selected. Seen in relation to the individual venture, lifecycle is anything but a law of nature.

25 Immortalised by Andy Grove (1996) CEO of Intel, the world's leading producer of microprocessors in his book, "Only the Paranoid Survive".

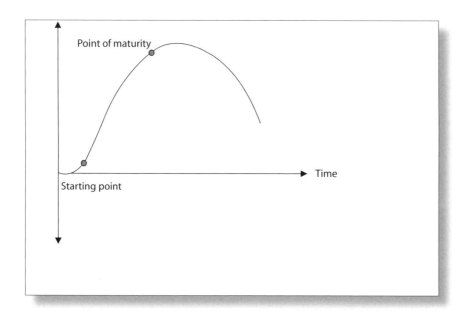

Figure 3.2 Lifecycle and inflection points

What is characteristic of the pioneering phase is that the market is unborn, nonexistent, uncultivated. In such a market there might be a supply of first-generation solutions, but often also uncertainty about utility, application, infrastructure, standards, service, social acceptance, needs and decisive selection criteria. The early solutions are often basic, generic, incomplete and functionally weak. Will the market grow? Will the innovation break through? Who will strike first?

The starting point is the phase in which the market takes off. It is the phase where competing technologies and concepts fight for prevalence and acceptance. Confusion reigns. Out of all the innovations it is only a small minority that will pass the inflection point, and even when this has occurred it is far from certain that the lifecycle of the individual product will resemble the one in Figure 3.6 – despite any positive development of the overall market.

During the early stages of the market, as it moves towards the possible but unknown inflection point, there are special opportunities for entrepreneurs. Not only because flexibility, speed, adaptability, and an opportunistic approach will be an efficient strategic pattern of reaction in view of the incalculability of the situation. But often also because the established suppliers, who should in principle be conquering the virgin market, overlook or underestimate the

84

opportunity, are hampered by technological and corporate-culture barriers, or simply define their business in a far too product orientated way. Everyone knows that the railway companies did not enter the motor car industry which, in turn, did not enter the airplane industry, which did not enter network computing.

The more radically innovative and discontinuing the uncultivated market is the more open is the window of opportunity to new entrepreneurial ventures. Nobody knows what will happen or when.

Will SoftPhone have its breakthrough or not (2004)?

Over the last 50 years, telephones have grown smarter. Push-buttons have replaced the dial. Many domestic phones are now cordless and have built-in memories and are increasingly equipped with a cordless headset. Not to mention mobile telecommunications that has really swept the world off its feet. One of its effects, among so many others, is that it has changed our perception of a telephone for collective use into an indispensable piece of personal property. But who says that it is even necessary to have a gadget like a telephone to cover one's communications requirements simply and cheaply?

Internet Protocol (IP) means that the user can replace the telephone with a computer combined with a (cordless) headset: a so-called SoftPhone. Same functionality, far cheaper and a lot of extras. SoftPhone breaks the frames of our perception of how verbal telecommunication is effected. Will it be a hit? Will SoftPhone pass the starting point? Are consumers going to accept a non-telephone?

The belief that a new market will arise and start to grow quickly, is not just a matter of capturing new knowledge and transforming it into a stand-alone commercial opportunity a little more swiftly or cleverly than others. Many promising breakthroughs never attain the growth rates prophesied because *crucial utility for consumers* – the exceptional value – is really missing. Satisfying needs often presupposes the establishment of an overall chain of supply and, therefore, of value. Depending on the specific conditions of the industry it does, in other words, take many simultaneous ventures before a specific market starts to accelerate in order both to stimulate demand across segments and to create genuine utility for the individual customer.

This is hardly a view that will surprise many practitioners. Nevertheless, it does contain an important factor for the entrepreneur to keep in mind: is it a good or a bad sign that you seem to be all alone in believing in the birth of a new market? Great opportunity – great risk? And the other way around: is an attractive but overpopulated future market by definition a good thing? Smaller risk – smaller opportunity? Inflection points brought about by fundamental technological leaps with many ramifications and, correspondingly, many derived innovations or entirely new product categories arising will normally constitute a good terrain for the entrepreneur, although there are negative points. One explanation is that the barriers to entry can be relatively low during this phase of market development. Nobody as yet owns the market positions, and well consolidated brands are losing their natural protection and leave the way open for newcomers if they are slow to discover and take possession of the new technology.

Think, for instance, of Brother (typewriters) or Facit (mechanical calculators) that did not manage to jump on the digital express in time. Or WordPerfect (text processing) when Windows replaced DOS. Instead companies and brands like Dell, Texas Instruments and Microsoft became the dominant players alongside existing brands like IBM and HP that did manage to change.

Increased innovation speed and efficient dissemination of knowledge mean that the product lifecycle is compressed and that *time-to-market* becomes a critical success factor. The inflection point at which the market growth rate starts to decline – the transition from growth to *maturity* – can in certain situations be a phase of extraordinary opportunities for entrepreneurship. At first sight this may seem illogical. When the growth rate is declining, it is well known that competition will intensify in the shape of enhanced product differentiation, price reduction, growing communicative pressure, vertical integration, in other words, higher barriers to entry.

The signal of the maturity point of declining growth indicates that the most innovative customers, who might chose new ways to maintain their desire for product differentiation, whether driven by taste or by competition – in other words, that a new market is arising elsewhere.

Tourist destinations that become too popular will see that pioneer travellers and well- off members of society look for other destinations – the window of opportunity opens up for other locations.

Don't forget your elephant task of the day

Time Manager has become a fantastic international business success. It all began in 1975 with the introduction of the Time Manager which was launched as a course in combination with a target orientated planning tool. The background philosophy was that people should learn how to manage their time. Concepts like pine needles, fish eagles or ospreys, the elephant task of the day, key areas were taught and learned at courses where, at the same time, the participants began using their Time Managers.

Time Manager went for business executives and was a hit. This indirectly was the starting signal for all the employees in a company – high and low – now having to control their (working) lives by means of the Time Manager. Shared experience, shared attitude, shared language.

Not many years later, during the process of diffusion, Time Manager lost its hold over top echelon managers – a qualitative inflection point. The elite looked for new I-orientated themes such as meditation and survival courses.

Time Manager chose to react to change by expanding internationally rather than figuring out new ideas for top managers – and achieved impressive results over the next 20 years.

3.6 From opportunity to congregation

Typically, entrepreneurs build their business idea on the notion that it is *their* invention, concept technology or solution which will activate latent, unmet needs and create a market. That the innovation is *the* key to the market.

The arguments can be very convincing – the list of benefits to the customers lengthy and important. Such entrepreneurs foresee an annoying, but surmountable sales problem as the only obstacle on the way, and think that sales competency can be bought in the market as a more or less standardised service.

These talented engineering projects should always be asked to define their *congregation*. In this connection a congregation is one segment or one target group, who cannot live without the innovation and will therefore embrace it unconditionally, and will become the evangelists of the new venture. To put it slightly polemically: chances without a congregation can be compared to opening a new shop without any customers. The congregation is exactly the needs and customers that the entrepreneur had in mind during the development process. The window of opportunity will only be coaxed open if you know who is the congregation. The founder of Time Manager knew that his congregation was the stressed out top manager who needed to manage his time better. The founders of Pressalit decided that the new pressed material should focus on one specific need – despite the fact that the material could have been used for many other purposes for which it could well have replaced existing technology. 50 years down the road, Pressalit is still focusing on the congregation. Only with time, it has grown bigger and more sophisticated.

Many entrepreneurs (mistakenly) believe that chances of success will grow the more customer segments and fields of application can be pointed to as potentially interesting and approachable. Consequently, most business plans include a thorough market analysis and a detailed segmentation model – but rarely a clear vision of a congregation. However, without congregation, the strategy will often become a butterfly strategy – fluttering from bloom to bloom. No nectar here? Off we go to the next one. Epitomised in statements like: Well, we could also … There are, of course, customers who …. Well, why don't we try to …. The transponder is a good case in point.

The difficult road of the transponder to the market

Around 1985 transponder technology was developed and led to a considerable number of entrepreneurial ventures. A transponder is a "gadget" made of metal about the size of a shirt button; by means of radio waves it can react to an individual data stream and pass on messages to the base station within a short range. The station can register the identity of the transponder and, accordingly, that of the object and can forward a steering impulse. The transponder was nothing less than a small revolution and the scopes of application were undreamed of. For instance, it would be possible to affix a transponder to all goods-wagons and mount base stations along railways in a sufficient number. In this way the railway company would always know where its stock was at any given time. Another idea was to sew transponders into work wear like overalls, smocks and uniforms. Many companies are responsible for equipping their staff with uniforms and are in charge of laundering them. There are indications that people were quite upset by having their clothes mixed up in the laundry with those of other people so that they did not get their own uniforms back. By means of transponders it would always be possible to identify the work clothes of each individual worker.

But it was in farming that the transponder really found its congregation. Pigs need different quantities of feed. The more accurately the farmer can measure the amount of feed for the individual pig, the higher the profit. Free range pigs mix a great deal among each other and this concept would generate a miserable operating profit unless the producer could keep track of each pig. With a transponder in each pig's ear and a receiver station at the feeding platform linked to a dosing unit, the producer can now automatically measure out a specific amount and mixture of feed for each individual animal. In addition, this can be combined with a weighing machine so that the producer can register the weight gain of each pig on a daily basis.

In pig production the transponder solution yielded a crucial added value in financial terms in contrast to the other interesting fields of application in which utility seemed more doubtful. You can never know for sure whether the congregation you have chosen is going to be receptive or rejective, or what it will take to remove resistance. Perhaps it is not even possible to determine whether you will be able gain the ear of the congregation you want.

Great Greenland

Some years ago Great Greenland re-launched the sealskin coat by means of a whole new design produced by a famous designer with the support of a massive advertising budget. 25 years before, on TV and in newspaper interviews – and the picture was shown all over the world -Brigitte Bardot, then a famous actress, had appealed to women to boycott sealskin coats because of the bloody slaughter of baby seals in Canada. Since then, no woman would be seen dead in a sealskin coat.

But now Great Greenland thought that the window of opportunity could be opened. And it could – well, sort of …. What emerged was a situation where the customers who bought sealskin coats were women of "a certain age" for whom a sealskin coat represented an unredeemed girlish dream of a prestigious fur coat. The congregation existed; it was ready, but its value as evangelists was negative – or at best, neutral.

Great Greenland should have steered the reintroduction of sealskin coats towards a congregation of trendsetters – famous artists, the royals, the jet set – through a mixture of exclusive distribution, communication, and prices that were many times higher.

But Nike did know its congregation.

Nike wins

The history of Nike's start is known to many people today: Phil Knight, the long distance runner and his coach, Bill Bowerman used Bowerman's wife's waffle iron and a bit of latex to develop a running shoe for long distance runners: it was lighter (value: faster times), more flexible (value: fewer blister, sprains and fractures) and had superior lateral stability (value: less risk of ankle injuries when running on an uneven surface).

At the time the overall market for running shoes was stagnating. Most people had one or two pairs of trainers and felt no need for more. But in the segment – long distance runners at elite level – the athletes loved Knight's and Bowerman's newly developed shoe, and their successes in competitions and championships later led to breakthroughs in tennis, basketball and other sports.

In terms of opportunity, what Knight and Bowerman saw was undoubtedly the chance to supply better quality, which certain customers (the congregation) would be in the market for and be willing to pay for it.

3.7 Window of opportunity paradoxes

Most entrepreneurial projects fail. Perhaps the market is *spurious* as was the case in the early days of e-commerce. Perhaps the market has *withered* and collapsed after a period of growth. Or perhaps a shake up occurs which eradicates all suppliers apart from a single one who follows the nature of the market, or as a result of a strategic gorilla game (Microsoft, Standard Oil, etc.). Perhaps from the beginning the window of opportunity was only open to that one player who is capable of developing a standard or the like.

The first and most serious problem is that the market turns out to be fundamentally "lousy", unreceptive and therefore impenetrable. The window of opportunity is closed despite consistent, uncontradicted rumours to the contrary. But what is it that happens when even talented entrepreneurial teams – even those backed by massive resources – still miscalculate and misunderstand the window of opportunity? One explanation may be that there are paradoxes at play, that is to say, phenomena and forces which seem illogical in many ways, difficult to explain or relatively unacceptable factors:

The paradox of innovative elevation

The more exciting and technologically advanced an idea is, the poorer its prognosis. Far-reaching ideas with new perspectives and paradigmatic potential are not bad because they are revolutionising, innovative or are being tried out for realisation in a newly started enterprise. Vision means strength. However, as already mentioned, great ideas tend to immunise their inventor from market signals. The process creating opportunities will therefore often be short of attention and flexibility to the wishes of customers. It is difficult to provide The Great Innovation with new insights, it is difficult to reformulate and modify it, and it is not always easy to realise it incrementally.

The paradox does not only have to do with exaggerated product orientation. However, precisely product orientation in combination with the high elevation may have as a result that risks linked to critical parts of the project course are overlooked.

The paradox of uniqueness

The more people who are competing to conquer the same market, the better will be the chances of succeeding for the individual.

But isn't the point to find a niche? To do everything to avoid a destructive race with competitors? That statistically a pioneer has a better chance of doing well? Yes, but the route to the niche – the unique position – nearly always travels via differentiation and also via competition and not the opposite. In time you can evolve towards a niche, but it is rare to be able to start in that way. For this reason it makes sense to go in search of those windows that many entrepreneurs are fighting to squeeze through. This does not mean de-focusing, but market orientation, enhanced demand stimulation and improved chances of calculated risk management.

The paradox of customer segments

The more interesting customer segments, the fewer prospective customers.

One loyal congregation is better than many interesting prospective customers. The image of the first customers as a congregation directs the venture towards imperatives, toward bridge heads so that the risk of repulsion is reduced as much as possible, such as Ecco Shoes and the comfortable fit.

The new enterprise is often weak in resources and cannot afford to remedy errors and start over. When there is only one bullet left in the chamber, you should never shoot into the herd.

The paradox of knowledge

The more received wisdom you possess, the less you know.

Knowledge and analytical competency is a two-edged sword. On the one hand, you will not go very far without well-defined competencies; knowledge is a prerequisite for successful innovation. On the other hand knowledge may hamper creativity and weaken market insight. Not even the cleverest people can analyse their way to the window of opportunity through logical reasoning. The magic of the moment will often make more of a difference than generic knowledge. Remember that none of the handsome, educated, clever suitors got the princess. Numskull Jack did it in the fairytale by Hans Christian Andersen by means of mud and a dead crow. A fairytale, to be sure, but the moral holds true into business life. The point was that Jack the Dullard was not ignorant, he was only underestimated. He possessed original knowledge as opposed to received and conventional wisdom and this enabled him to go against the great and the good. He was thinking in along positioning lines.

The paradox of the great changes

The greatest opportunity is embedded in small changes in market conditions.

Entrepreneurs tend to congregate in the slipstream of the great inventions and innovations. Innovations that move the world. This is far from a bad idea, but often it is far too obvious. The ability to combine two or more changes, or to understand small changes exhaustively often reflects a truly market orientated, receptive approach which, in turn, improves chances. The smallest things are often the most overlooked things, and they call for good eyesight.

The paradox of the importance of who you associate with

Peripheral personal networks provide more inspiration than intimate friends.

Many people think that your best friends are also your best source of inspiration and criticism. This idea may be wrong. The wider and more facetted the peripheral network of the entrepreneur is, the better will be the chance of creating and developing a business opportunity. Close friends might only give affirmation to the entrepreneur, avoid hurtful comments, and probably not supply a surprising impulse.

3.8 Inventory: Evaluation of the window of opportunity

In the inventory below, a number of measuring points and assertions about the window of opportunity have been identified. By comparing the statements to concrete entrepreneurial projects or the specific business idea, a deeper awareness of the legitimacy of the idea in the market can be developed.

The inventory is based on the conclusions and arguments that have been introduced and discussed above. The assessment of whether something is to be deemed a positive or negative indicator in relation to the window of opportunity may be an important signal for the new venture.

The idea behind the inventory is to improve the knowledge in a new business venture about its absolute point of strength. The inventory can be used individually or as a group tool. A quantitative score is not envisaged here.

	MEASURING POINTS AND INDICATORS	PLUS	NEUTRAL	MINUS	?
I	*Measuring Point: Shape of the window of opportunity*				
A	I understand the market better than anybody else and have mapped out clear, well defined needs in an unprecedented way. As such the opportunity has been identified by creative market insight. I still do not know what is required to solve the problem, but it is surmountable				
B	I have unique technological understanding and competency, and at the same time I am aware of all the perspectives and limitations of the technology. All I need to do is find more scope for the application. This must be in areas where customers are not afraid to choose new approaches, because it would be sensible to do so, and it would not cause disruption for them.				

C	I understand the market – customers and their needs – better than anybody else; furthermore I have a unique technology or competency. So let's go.				
D	Truthfully, I am not all that aware of the needs out there and not competency focused. But I have visions, I am stubborn, and in the end I will succeed				
II	**Measuring point: the aha-experience and its origin**				
A	There is no aha-experience, but there is a lot of room in this market				
B	I made a random discovery				
C	Things just came to me when I had worked my way through the material and the problems methodically				
D	When you are constantly on the lookout and use your senses, it is easier to stumble over something. That is what happened to me				
E	This is only my hobby. Interest was the prime mover. In this way, I discovered an entirely new opportunity				
III	**Measuring point: grid of opportunity**				
A	I will create exceptional, perceived value in one and only one of the six phases of the customer's cycle of experience: purchase, delivery, uses, supplement, maintenance and scrapping				
B	I will create exceptional, perceived value in one and only one of the six fields of value: productivity, simplification, convenience, risk, image, environmental friendliness				
C	I will apply the same utility factor, but in another phase of the customer's cycle of experience				

D	I will apply the same utility factor, but in the same phase of the customer's cycle of experience				
IV	**Measuring point: timing and lifecycle**				
A	Timing is crucial to the sustainability of the idea, and I am convinced my timing is correct				
B	I expect the starting point to be there shortly and that, subsequently, the market will grow fast				
C	The timing for this particular group of customers is perfect because of a point of maturity which means that their need is relatively unmet at the moment				
D	Timing is not crucial at all; the market will accept my solution no matter when it is introduced				
V	**Measuring point: congregation**				
A	I know exactly who our congregation is, and I keep my eye on it even though it is tempting to throw out the big net				
VI	**Measuring point: summary**				
A	Right now the window of opportunity is open to all, but only for a short time				
B	I am the only one, or nearly so, who has caught sight of the opportunity and I count on being more or less alone in this exciting market				
C	The window of opportunity has closed, but I expect that it will spring open on its own accord, and then it is important to be ready				
D	What will open the window of opportunity is my completely individual competency				

Evaluation of the window of opportunity

As a construction the concept of the window of opportunity is based on the notion of the exceptional, combined with the dynamic. Success requires both extreme customer focus and insight into relative competencies. The window of opportunity is primarily a metaphor aimed at practice – the acid test – on the road to creative market insight and idea for establishing the final concept.

Literature

Ardichivili Alexander, Lardozo Richard, Ray Sourav: *A Theory of Entrepreneurial Opportunity Identification and Development.* Journal of Business Venturing. 2000.

D'Aveni Richard A: *Hypercompetitive Rivalries – Competition in Highly Dynamic Environments.* The Free Press. N.Y. USA. 1995.

Deakins David, Freel Mark: *Entrepreneurship and small Firms.* Mc.Graw Hill Education. 2003.

Drucker Peter F*.: Innovation and Entrepreneurship – practice and principles.* Butterworth, London. 1986 (1999).

Drucker Peter F.: *The Discipline of Innovation.* Harvard Business Review, Nov-Dec 1998 s 149 – 156.

Franklin Carl: *Why innovations fail.* Spiro Press. London. 2003.

Harper David A*.: Entrepreneurship and the market process.* Rothledge. London. 1996.

Hills Gerald et alt: *Marketing and entrepreneurship research – ideas and opportunities.* Quorum books. Greenwood Press Weestport. Connecticut, US. 1994.

Mullins John W.: *The Business Road Test.* Prentice Hall. London. 2003.

Pearson Alan W. Ed. By Henry Jane, Walker David: *Managing Innovation: An Uncertainty Reduction process.* Sage Publications. London. UK. 1991.

Porter Michael E.: *Competitive Advantage – Creating and Sustaining Superior Performance.* Free Press. N.Y. 1985.

Porter Michael E.: *Competitive Strategy.* Free Press. N.Y. 1981.

Prahalad C.K og Hamel Gary: *Competing for the Future.* Harvard Business School Press. Boston. 1994.

Prahalad C.K. og Hamel Gary*: The Core Competence of the Corporation.* Harvard Business Review 1990.

Times Jeff. A.: *New Venture Creation – Entrepreneurship for the 21.st Century.* Mc.Graw Hill. 1990.

Tushman Michael L., Anderson Philip: *Managing Strategic Innovation and Change – a Collection of Readings.* Oxford University Press. 1997.

4. Creation of the business concept

> "We sell dreams, deliver experiences and deposit memories."
>
> *Chairman Simon Spies, Spies Travels Tours*

The creative market insight of the entrepreneur and the discovery of the window of opportunity bring forward the new venture to the business definition itself. The creation of the business concept means to think out and shape the unique offer, i.e. what service to provide to whom, how and why. It is a question of the degree of differentiation and focusing as well as of direction.

The design of the business concept will determine whether the meeting between market and opportunity will be positive further down the line. The concept is the coalescence of the opportunity itself. The concept determines the choice of product not the other way around.

In this chapter a dynamic template is introduced; it can be used to establish, process and validate a business definition seen from the point of view of customers. Not that customers are necessarily right, but because they are in charge of deciding. This chapter also takes up the conflicts, trade offs and risks that any new entrepreneurial venture will come up against.

In accordance with the market orientated approach of *The Business Idea*, the basic notion of the chapter is that in many cases the business definition is *the* key to success for the new enterprise rather than the product idea.

4.1 How to define a business

How often have we not heard the question asked, "Which business are we in?" when a discussion is getting stuck or is to be brought back on track along the path of an entrepreneurial process. Unfortunately, it is not very often that anyone actually goes up to the blackboard to give a clear, simple and convincing answer that everybody understands and can wholeheartedly endorse. The explanation is very simple: the business definition is the very secret.

The classic example of the recession-hit American railways of the 1950s, which defined their business in a product orientated way (railway) rather than in a market orientated way (transport) for better or worse illustrates the challenge. On the one hand, the narrow, technology based business definition took the railways into deep recession because customers left them for aircraft and motorcars. On the other hand, the business value of seeing railway operation as transport would be virtually zero because this business definition is too abstract and generic. It cannot be manoeuvred managerially. The formulation of a convincing business definition and its conceptualisation, therefore, constitutes the backbone of entrepreneurship. It encompasses the synthesis of market and opportunity insight (what is feasible?), competency profile (what is achievable for us?) and objective (what do we want?). In most cases the business idea must be considered the core of innovation – the very discovery of the opportunity.

IKEA is a brilliant example of an enterprise which attempts to unify many considerations into its business definition.

The IKEA business definition: democratisation

An excerpt from the will and testament of a furniture dealer:

"Once and for all we have decided to be on the side of the many. What is good for our customers is, in the long run, also good for us. This is a goal that requires commitment.

In all states and in all social systems … an over-proportionate share of resources is used to satisfy a small fraction of the population. In our industry, much too much of what is beautiful and new is reserved for a small group of rich people. This fact has contributed to the formulation of our objective …

A well-known Swedish industrialist has said that IKEA has meant more to the process of democratisation than the total sum of political decisions … From the outset much of what is new was created for the majority of the people – for all those who have limited resources. We are in the lead of this development….

The things we use to achieve our objective are all characterised by our different line and our endeavour to be simple and straight-forward in the way we deal with each other and our environment. Lifestyle is a strong word, but I don't hesitate to use it. To have a better everyday life, you need also to be able to liberate yourself from status and conventions – to be a free man or woman.

It is our goal to turn ourselves into a concept in this field, too, for our own sake and to give inspiration to the world around us … "

Grand rhetoric about pinewood furniture and with a clear message: If you wish to serve a mass market in an industry characterised by craft methods what it takes is industrial thinking without compromising good design.

Ventures of the problem solving kind aimed at well defined needs (see Chapter 3) need not worry too much about defining the business. The research group of pharmaceutical enterprise which develops an efficient, cheap treatment of AIDS might possibly have to choose between different business models, just as the product development process is incredibly difficult; a group of researchers or a small research based firm is likely to choose a different business concept from the one chosen by a global pharmaceuticals producer. But the difficulty about the nature of the perceived problem and the character of the market opportunity, seems clear from the outset.

If an idea is imitative on the basis of the motto, "there is always room for one more," the fact is that others have done the job of defining the business.

However, the market innovative project often consists of a cocktail in which the problem, need, opportunity and competency are processed more or less iteratively in the search for a sustainable business concept; here the discussion of "which business do we want to be in," is extremely relevant. Is it the business definition itself that constitutes the *advantage* of the venture or does it arise as *a matter of course*? If the latter is the case, this may indicate that the concept needs to be put through another round of grinding in the concept mill.

Experience shows that the most common trap for the entrepreneur to fall into is that of inverse logic. When you have reached the point in strategy formulation at which the business concept is to be defined, you are already locked into a production concept, a platform, a method. Since the product, the technology and the method are unique along this special dimension, the business needs to be defined in this special way. Conceptual creativity is weakened and the freedom to establish the business definition *itself* as the secret weapon of the future enterprise is restricted.

You cannot claim that market definition and business idea is one and the same thing, although the distinction between market and concept is sometimes blurred. In the hi-fi market, Bang & Olufsen and Sony, for example, define their concepts completely differently from one another. In the market for wrist watches the conceptual span goes from buy-and-discard over bijouterie, via digital management, to jewel concepts and luxury brands. The rapid breakthrough of package holidays was quite a different story. In this field history was made when market, notion and concept were fused together.

Sangria Party – Olé!

The two rivals in the Scandinavian tour operating business, Eilif Krogager, the vicar-turned-tour-operator from the village of Tjæreborg, and Simon Spies, psychologist and eccentric were package tour operating pioneers. In the 1950s and early 1960s ordinary people began to have more leisure time and higher purchasing power as a consequence of the industrial revolution of the post-war-years. Energetic entrepreneurs as they were, they began organising coach trips for groups to nearby countries, but soon caught sight of the chance to create a completely new type of business: charter tours to Southern Europe. They saw a bigger market, increasing holiday consumption, a craving for the sun, parties and fun as well as achievable prestige for a broad customer segment. They created a price corridor by means of economies of scale, industrial production in air transport, high capacity utilisation, etc, so that ordinary north Europeans could afford a week or two annually in Spain. They created a package product with freedom from problems, a feeling of safety and companionship – the blessings and extension of the welfare state translated into sunny Spanish beaches and Pesetas at a low rate of exchange. A major success had been born. Whereas the leading travel agents of the day had defined their business as individual, made-to-order trips for the well-to-do, the entrepreneurs Spies and Tjæreborg produced standardised tours on a mass scale at low prices for ordinary people whose, hitherto impossible dreams were now fulfilled. The IKEA of the travel business were victorious.

Spies and Tjæreborg created a new business concept and managed to out-manoeuvre a well established industry which was accustomed to higher margins and another clientele.

When new product markets arise, you will often be a witness to a legitimacy race along the following lines: Which closely related industries will have existing business definitions that permit, or even demand, that firms attempt to conquer the new market And what is the relative strength of new entrepreneurial ventures and existing enterprise claiming the market?

100

Around 2000, the international marine authority, IMO, decided that all vessels carrying passengers should be equipped with a black box like in aircraft; this box is known as a Voyage Data Recorder. A VDR is to collect data from alarms, fire doors, the bridge, radar, etc. and is to be mounted on the roof of the vessel. It must be capable of resisting extreme impacts from heat, pressure, explosions and bumps. Overnight, the IMO order created a global VDR market worth over $100 million annually – an obvious entrepreneurial opportunity. In quick succession around 10 to 15 suppliers launched VDR solutions and began a headlong race for market shares. Interestingly enough, a complete newcomer, who had anticipated the birth of the market, snatched a significant share of the market, but at the same time had to agree to constricting distribution and marketing agreements to gain access. Producers of black boxes for aircraft also thought that the shipping market was a natural part of their business definition and that they could make an immediate transfer of all critical competencies from aircraft products. Their strength was their incontestable technological level and their brand equity, but they were short of customer access and sales channels; added to this was the perception that their products were very costly.

In addition manufacturers of nautical instruments like radars, integrated bridge systems, etc., naturally considered the VDR market to be their domain and as a natural product line extension. Same group of customers, same distribution, same basic technology – mechanical design, hardware and software. Also some big shipyards saw the opportunity to penetrate the VDR market. Why? Because it is in connection with their annual shipyard overhaul that VDRs are installed onboard vessels. Some chose to buy key components, for instance the very important casing or software from strategic sub-suppliers. The sub-suppliers, consequently, defined their business differently, but were part of the value chain. Other VDR manufacturers designed and produced turnkey solutions themselves.

The battle for the VDR market is not yet over. The sudden expansion of the market initially created a friendly competitive climate with room for most players. Industry consolidation can be expected to take place when market growth rates start declining.

Defining and conceptualising the business if you are a young innovative business venture is rarely an easy management task – just look at the VDR market. It is tempting, but rarely advisable, to trust your own product competency exclusively. Nor is there any guarantee that you will be the first in the market or, conversely, that you can squeeze your way in hoping that it is true that there is always room for one more. However, it is possible to process the issue systematically; it is a matter of opportunities, competencies and objectives.

4.2 The three main tracks of the business concept[26]

For whom? What with? How? These short questions, the answers to which are rarely obvious, reflect the three dimensions or main tracks that the entrepreneur may follow to shape her business definition, viz.: *Customer group* (who), *function* (what) and *technology* (how). Establishing your customer group is about segmentation of the market, i.e. a subdivision of customers into groups on the basis of differences in their needs, and on that basis selecting one or more target groups – the congregation. Products and services carry out certain functions for a customer. Function should conceptually be distinct from the *way* in which the function is carried out (the technology) and from the utility to the customer, which may vary considerably.

Functions may be *complementary* in relation to activities or systems – for instance, loading and unloading. Functions may be said to be *uniform* in those cases where the execution of one function is virtually identical with another: transportation from A to B compared with transportation from C to D. Finally, functions may be *non-related* in those cases where there is no connection between meeting one customer need and other needs. Technologies describe alternative ways in which a particular function can be executed for a customer. In the case of transportation: by means of aircraft, trains, trucks or vessels.

At first sight, it may seem a purely academic exercise to keep all three tracks open at the same time when the entrepreneurial venture moves from idea to business concept because at least one, and often two, of the dimensions are given beforehand. For example, many ventures see the light of day because the entrepreneur has developed a promising, innovative technology that would now like to see it commercialised. Would it not be absurd if the final business

---

26 Inspired by Abell (1979.1980)

definition had as a result that the technology as a solution would have to be scrapped? No, why would it be absurd, if the project does arrive at a promising and robust business definition anyhow?

Markets are heterogeneous and dynamic arenas in which the business definition is a decisive strategic competitive tool. In any market there is a number of different business concept and, as such, divergent market delineations. An example is outlined below.

Customer Relationship Management

In the market for Customer Relationship Management systems suppliers do not at all define their businesses in the same way despite the fact that they are competing for the same customers. ERP[27] suppliers with SAP, Oracle and Microsoft as the most important ones, cover many functions that have a relatively broad customer spectrum. CRM is part of the total functionality they offer, and compatibility is one of their strongest sales arguments. Conversely, specialised CRM firms – the best known one is probably Siebel – concentrate on one single function and has a broad potential customer focus. The advantages of these suppliers are their specific CRM solution, their expertise and their depth.

The third type of player has seen wireless communication as an important possible expansion of the CRM market. Suppliers of mobile CRM target their development and services at a somewhat narrower group of customers (companies with many travelling employees) and with a somewhat narrower spectrum of functions, due to, among other factors, bandwidth and security. Their business is defined as technological peak competency for transferring knowledge about wireless communication to the CRM market. This snapshot has other interesting facets, viz. lifecycle and complementarity. The market for administrative ERP systems is older than the CRM industry and partly, is one of its prerequisites, as financial-administrative data from ERP is used in CRM solutions.

The example in figure 4.1 illustrates the strategic room for manoeuvre in the formulation of new business concepts that require a deep insight into the contents and meaning of the three axes or spheres of opportunity.

---

27 Enterprise Resource Planning

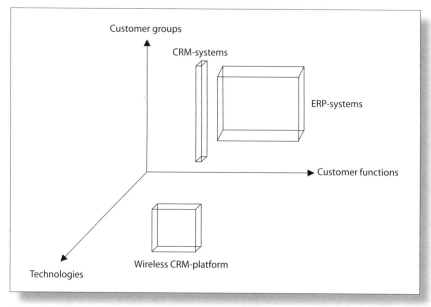

Figure 4.1 An example of the three dimensions of the business definition – CRM

4.3 A business definition typology

Customer group, customer function and technology constitute the basic dimensions that an entrepreneur has to process very thoroughly. Partly, to understand the *total market*, partly to pinpoint the part of the market wishing to be served and – most importantly – to be able to decide the way in which the new enterprise should position itself.

In the simultaneous processing of the questions about whom, with what and how, opportunities, competency profiles, ideas, and objectives are confronted and combined into a hypothesis about, "which business do we want to be in". In other words: how do we view the (partial) market we want to conquer? And how do we want the conquest to be and why?

For a moment let us look at worldwide corporations like Sony and Honda. They do not define their business as entertainment electronics and means of transport when they are to explain their unique offer, but rather as minimalisation and small engines respectively. Or the Scandinavian Airline System (SAS) which in its heyday defined itself as the "businessman's airline" and set up the business system of the company in accordance with this particular customer group.

These examples illustrate the *business definitions* in relation to the three basic dimensions, customer group, function and technology *as well as* in relation to the *business concepts* of the enterprises. Sony: differentiation aimed at a broad market achieved by means of different technology and functional orientation. Honda: differentiation with a considerable width as regards consumer and function selection, but a much stronger technology than that of its competitors. SAS: focusing on specific customer groups with virtually the same functional and technological profile as that of its competitors.

Thus, differentiation and focus are key concepts that are to be interwoven with the three basic dimensions to form a typology for business definitions:

- *A focused business concept* means that the new venture chooses to concentrate on one single basic dimension and a single one of its attributes – for example, a specific customer group, function or technology (also see the Grid of opportunity in Chapter 3).
- *A differentiated business concept* for a new venture means a concept with a broad market appeal and differentiation in a single dimension or more compared to the competitors.
- *An undifferentiated business concept* means that the new enterprise defines its business broadly in relation to the three basic dimensions while at the same time it does not differentiate its way of doing business compared to its competitors or across customer segments.

This brings us the following typology:

Sources of business definition:	Focused	Differentiated	Undifferentiated
Customer group			
Function			
Technology			

Table 4.1 A typology for defining business area and business concept[28]

Source: Inspired by Abell (1979-1980)

---

28 See also Kotler's three marketing strategies: Differentiated, undifferentiated and focused as functions of factors such as: Resources (limited resources indicate focuses/concentrated), product-market homogeneity (the more so, the more factors speak in favour of an undifferentiated concept), early stage lifecycle (early phases speak in favour of an undifferentiated approach) as well as the strategies of competitors.

One cannot in all seriousness suggest a single, universal recipe for what is best, and when it is best for the individual project. In the early stages of lifecycle, the needs of customers are often fairly similar, and the technological degrees of freedom correspondingly restricted, something which speaks in favour of an undifferentiated business definition – just think of the early generations of mobile phones.

In later stages, the market is split into segments and the different needs emerge more clearly; similarly a more refined technology emerges – something that reinforces differentiation.

Typically, entrepreneurs have fewer resources at their disposal than an established company. This indicates that a concentrated business definition – focused or differentiated – may turn out to be advantageous.

New business ventures are sometimes trapped into thinking that *more* is automatically perceived as *better*. Many entrepreneurs think that the justification for their business concept is precisely their ability to deliver more. That the customers will appreciate more is better. This is why they go through a great deal of trouble to develop product properties whose unique feature is more and therefore assumed to be better: power-to-performance key figures for chips, algorithms, which use less energy, platforms with stronger interfaces, applications with broader scope, speed measured in nanoseconds in real time, extra functionality in software, compatibility, flexibility, etc. Nevertheless they are often disappointed and surprised by the unreceptiveness of the customers when the products are first introduced.

If so many entrepreneurs run into this *quality paradox*, it may be due to the way in which the cross field between business differentiation and product differentiation is handled. The business concept illustrates the entrepreneur's solution, which is intended to lead to an extremely high degree of need satisfaction for certain customers compared to the existing solutions in the market. If higher specifications of product characteristics do not lead to greater utility, the explanation has to be either that the customers feel that the higher specifications are relatively unimportant, or that the concept is not aimed specifically enough at those very customer segments that are technically advanced and would therefore appreciate these product properties. Or – and this is a very important point – the explanation might be that in its concept formulation the future enterprise is incapable of communicating the way in which these superior product properties will generate exceptional value for a customer compared to their *total opportunity costs.*[29]

The three basic dimensions and market approaches together form the fields of the business definition, and the business definition is not identical with one specific product.

Dafolo: from form printer to digital administration 24/7

In a little over 45 years, the Danish company Dafolo has changed from being a printing house specialising in printing municipal administrative forms into an enterprise that takes public administration into the e-age with digital dialogue systems for improved contact between authorities and citizens.

At the time of its start in 1957, the owner Johannes Ellitsgaard had forms printed at a local printing firm and kept his stock at his family home. A few years down the road, Dafolo had purchased its first printing machine and built its own premises.

Form printing was supplemented with the printing of law books and manuals. The number of machines grew and so did the building, and slowly but surely EDP made its way into the graphic work processes. The reorganisation of local authorities in Denmark in 1970 boosted demand substantially, and Dafolo had to expand once again.

In the 1980s, Dafolo began developing computer programmes for administrative purposes, and in the 1990s the enterprise introduced electronic forms.

In parallel with this development the enterprise's competencies in the field of graphic printing was supplemented with know-how about communication, presentation and competence development in public organisations.

In 2000, Dafolo presented plans for the first comprehensive solution for digital administration, and a large-scale project for the digitalisation of three municipalities was initiated.

This is truly the grand opening of the digital age facilitating direct contact between citizens and municipalities over the Internet 24 hours a day. In return,

---

29 Opportunity costs in the sense of what the new concept costs and the loss suffered by the customer in phasing out his existing solution.

the number of printing presses has been reduced and the darkrooms have been replaced by computers.

From the very first form up to the 24-hour digital administration venture, the leitmotif has been consistent: developing and selling solutions, which, with the technology available at any time, make the best contributions to administrative simplification and improved dialogue.

"Which business are we in?" Dafolo was, and still is, specialising in supplying flexible, efficient administrative solutions to municipalities. Dafolo does not define its business as supplying forms, although the product and supreme money spinner for the company for many years was the design and production of paper forms. Dafolo focuses on one specific customer group and on specific functions in that customer group. The original innovation of the company was really a technological push, whereas transition to digital administration – a totally different medium 35 years later – should more correctly be described as demand pull.

The fact that it is possible to let core products lapse altogether is demonstrated by Volkswagen's decision to phase out the Beetle, the Bubble Teaser. The cult product beyond all other cult products. The Beetle was the epitome of the Volkswagen works, the soul of the company, the world's most popular car ever, and the soul of German manufacturing culture. The decision generated intensely negative reactions from all points of the compass.[30] But who thinks of that today with the Ludo, the Polo, the Golf and Passat having created new brand positions for the company.

DDH – the Society for Moorland Reclamation

In 1866 a group of forward looking men, led by E.M. Dalgas, took an initiative which was to be of major importance to the development of Danish society as we know it today.

With the establishment of the DDH, the foundations were laid for an enterprise that initially made a major effort to make the Danish moorland

---

30 The Beetle was redesigned and re-launched and was only discontinued completely in 2003.

fertile, which is the reason for the Danish name of the company Det Danske Hedeselskab. With this cultivation process followed activities in the fields of meadow irrigation and plantation of woods and hedges and, in this way, the Society produced an important societal development. For most of the time the Society has existed, its functional and success criterion was to reshape original landscapes into arable land and taming the forces of nature like sand drift and flooding.

Over the last 30 years, the objective has been turned around 180 degrees and is now the restablishment of original landscapes, landscape and environment protection and forestation.

Although it might look that way, the business definition of the DDH has not really changed in the course of its history. If the business concept had been product specific (reclamation of new arable land at the expense of nature), the Society would have died. However, because the functions of the DDH (hedges, forestation) and its technology (landscape planning) are the pillars, the Society has thrived. The business definition of the DDH is not the protection of agriculture, but the protection of landscapes.

The table below is a schematic overview which provides a spectrum of strategic formulae that make it possible to (re)define a business.

Strategies for (re)defining	Focus or differentiation through:		
	Customer group	Customer functions	New technology
1	Same	Same	Different
2	Same	Different	Same
3	Different	Same	Same
4	Same	Different	Different
5	Different	Different	Same
6	Different	Same	Different
7	Different	Different	Different

Table 4.2 Innovative business definitions/redefinitions compared to the established players in the market

Source: Inspired by Abell (1979-1980).

The typology looks frighteningly schematic: a kind of square list of correct answers. Before arriving at a business definition, the entrepreneur has carried out creative segmentation and has discovered the window of opportunity; he knows his customer and their needs, the decisive purchase criteria, the counterpoints, his own competencies, the gap between needs and abilities, etc. Figure 4.3 is one among several checkpoints for the exact business definition, represented by the following four questions:

- Which of the seven strategies for redefining does the new venture use?
- What are the customers' obvious, essential and decisive decision criteria in the purchasing process?
- Why, how or when is the "offer" differently unique for the customers when confronted with their selection criteria?
- What type of competitor is at play: multi market/multi product; customer centred, function specialised, etc.?

4.4 Market boundaries and entrepreneurial opportunities

Markets change (see Chapter 2). Not just in terms of size, but also in terms of structure and driving forces. There are many and complex reasons for this. Some reasons are predictable, others are random. Some are triggered by demand factors, others by the supply side, and others again are caused by external factors. For example, the innovation represented by the business venture itself.

Such changes constitute fertile entrepreneurial ground. They create special opportunities for new ideas and entrepreneurship. Market development can be explained by changes in the three basic dimensions, therefore, by understanding and predicting essential shifts in the basic dimensions, the entrepreneur gains an insight into the forces that may trigger new opportunities. This can be illustrated in the following.

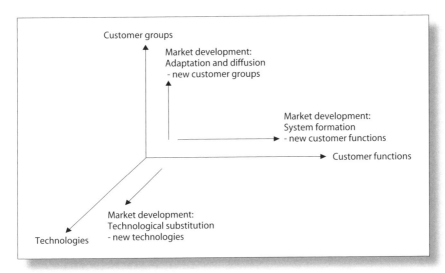

Figure 4.2 Market development in three dimensions

Source: Inspired by Abell (1979-1980)

Product lifecycle (primarily generated by demand) is the graphic presentation of the diffusion process, but cannot as such explain market developments caused by new customer functions or technology shifts (primarily generated by supply).

Spies and Tjæreborg exploited *market development* when new groups of customers began demanding trips to the exotic destinations of the time. Many years later, Marco Polo established a solid business in developing new customer functions for existing customer segments – arduous treks on horseback across the Andes.

Cultura produced by Arla is an excellent example of *system formation* in a fast moving consumer goods market. Cultura is an innovative development of yoghurt as a snack. By packaging the yoghurt with a multi-sprinkle in a special glued-on pouch as well as a plastic spoon that will fold out, the product replaced several separate functions.

In reality, market development follows all the three axes at the same time. Well established suppliers often have a better chance of holding on to their position if only one dimension is changed – new customer groups, extra features, or new standards. The chance of creating sustainable new business concepts increases in step with turbulence, and the more all three dimensions change or can be changed at the same because the well established players are tied to chains of supply and locked positions.

Dell Direct

In the course of a few years, Dell has become a great global success and a world brand. Dell's annual sales exceed $35 billion and the company has nearly 40,000 employees.

The Dell business concept is simple: Dell sells computers direct to the end users without any intermediaries that would only make the product more expensive, delay delivery and confuse customers. Dell sells computers made to order, i.e. the customers can configure and specify – tailor – their own personal solution. Dell has developed into the most cost effective supplier and for that reason the company is very price competitive.

Dell was founded in 1984 in Austin, Texas. With the breakthrough of the Internet ten years later, market access grew almost explosively.

Dell exploited a parallel market development in all three dimensions. Massive new customer segments came onto the computer market within a relatively short time: private households, small and medium-size enterprises, and students at all levels. Dell created a new technology, the Lego-block system, without delaying deliveries, and Dell introduced a new function by way of the direct contact with consumers.

The dominant players could not imitate Dell. Their go-to-market model went via distributors and dealers. Advance stocks of finished products eliminated any chance of producing to order. The many links in the chain of supply led to high costs and long transports. Any imitative action would make the dealership link change their supplier and brand immediately – in other words a ferocious threat of cannibalisation.

What is Dell's business concept? Direct sale of computers? Production built to order and individualisation? Could the concept be extended to television sets? Consumer electronics? Mobile phones? Furniture?

The business definition and the market boundaries are like Siamese twins. Inseparable. A reciprocal precondition. Parallel, not sequential. The best weapon of the strong venture consists in creative market insight translated into an innovative business definition. The venture introduces completely new market boundaries (Dell). Market boundaries become the result of entrepreneurship, not its cause. Markets differ. Successful, innovative entry into the existing market by means of business redefinition or through opportunist exploitation of a market development along one or more of the three basic dimensions require in-depth knowledge of the strategies which are, at the moment, operative in the market in question in relation to the basic dimension as well as the degree of differentiation or focus.

In some situations entrepreneurial thinking may lead to a reformulation of market boundaries. The principal types of such a possibility can be seen in table 4.3:

Market type	Characteristics:	Possibility of redefinition:	Examples:
Customer focused	• Market governed by needs • All suppliers focusing on certain customer groups • Differentiated/ undifferentiated/focused strategies	• Technological innovation combined with the discovery of new customer groups/needs	• Amusement parks. Amusements for children becoming amusements for adults
Function specialised	• Market governed by values • Competitors over-focusing on certain functions	• Function expansion combined with customer focus and different technology	• From cleaning to security service • Fine food restaurants in fashion shops
Technology dictated	• Exploitation market • All feel bound by the properties of certain technologies • Differentiated/ undifferentiated/focused Strategies	• New applications and combinations • Concept innovation	• Multimedia shows

Table 4.3 Some market types and market boundaries – the entrepreneur's chance

Even mature, very competitive markets can be extremely well suited for entrepreneurs, if it becomes possible to find one's way to unique market approaches that might have – but do not necessarily have to have – their roots in profound technological change or lengthy and diffuse product development.

Markets with relatively satisfied suppliers and very uniform thinking sometimes constitute interesting opportunities for creative entrepreneurs. This is how the United Exhibits Group saw the light of day.

Missing Link Alive

In 1984 Teit Ritzau, a physician and film director, had the chance of showing a holographic exhibition at Tivoli Gardens in Copenhagen, Denmark.

This became the starting signal for the United Exhibits Group, an enterprise which, 15 years down the road, has an annual turnover of nearly €7 million, offers nice profits, and holds a global market position with 20 shows touring the globe.

The mission of the company is to create and produce scientifically plausible exhibitions with unique angles; to some extent a museum concept. Missing Link Alive tells the story of the first human beings on earth from the perspective of development history. The Dawn of Human Spirit zooms in on the early artistic and intellectual endeavours of man – cave paintings, etc. The Quest for Immortality tells the history of ancient Egypt. Chinamania will be launched in connection with China hosting the Olympics of 2008 and tells the story of how the Middle Empire was united thousands of years ago; it is estimated that this exhibition will be seen by nearly 100 million people.

United Exhibition involves the world's leading scientists, scholars and museum experts in its product development ensuring the highest level of expertise, the rarest approaches and irrefutable scholarly validity. The exhibitions take up the most important scientific and cultural events of human history and provide modern people with an opportunity to see something unique. The exhibitions are rich in effects, multimedia and things you can touch. They are interactive, entertaining – using special effects from the film industry. Edutainment. The exhibitions are held at the world's biggest, most prestigious museums and exhibition centres.

Why was it an entrepreneurial initiative and not the museum industry itself that expanded the boundaries of and redefined the business? Somewhat simplified we might say that all museums are dictated by the same, focused exhibition technology, the notion of what it is you do as a museum, and especially what you do not do. Although museums are undergoing radical renewal, they have not stretched the business concept far enough, quickly enough, conceptually enough.

4.5 Factors influencing business definition and concept design

What, at the end of the day, the market will allow in terms of what, seen in isolation, is achievable for a new entrepreneurial venture is affected by several factors. Factors that must be subjected to a close, cognitive analysis and that must be implanted into the business definition which an entrepreneur ultimately chooses. The factors are not necessarily to be seen as restrictions and thus entry barriers. But the consideration of fundamental conditions and forces in the market are inherent to any entrepreneurial project.

Three of the most important ones should be mentioned, viz.:

- Buying behaviour
- Resource and competency requirements
- Cost relations

Buying behaviour

Insight into buying behaviour automatically leads to creative market insight.

Buying behaviour varies and is a science of its own. Developing a business idea which is compatible with the buying behaviour of some or all customers presupposes an awareness of the organisation of decision criteria in the procurement process.

We distinguish between four levels in industrial procurement processes: the strategic, the technical, the commercial and the transactional levels.[31] In practice the problem is that the procurement department is far more systems orientated – strategically/technically – than would seem justified by the specific product market. This complicates penetration considerably.

Buyers normally have a preference for fewer, bigger well known suppliers rather than the opposite as this is assumed to lead to higher overall efficiency and better interaction between constituent parts and partial services bought in.[32]

One consequence of this inertia on the part of the buyers and their tendency towards conservatism is that newly established enterprises will benefit from positioning themselves back in the value chain rather than well forward. *Price sensitivity* is another central aspect of the conceptual considerations. Often you will be surprised at the low sensitivity to economic rationales of some business customers, because of which they are more or less immune to new offers despite

---

31 Nielsen and Wilke (1999)

32 An argument that does not seem to run counter to the trend towards unbundling and in-sourcing of components rather than package deals; many enterprises, rightly, feel that the price they pay for package solutions is too high (photocopier + service and maintenance contracts).

the fact that the investment calculations look very convincing. Examples: e-learning solutions with high effect on learning economics, reductions in time-to-market, etc.; virtual online product configuration leading to massive manpower reductions; software that increases salespeople's efficiency considerably. Far less costly but, at the very least, equally as efficient technical platforms as the ones customers are now using; however, resistance to new media and procedures tends to be stronger than financial calculations on their own.

It is rarely difficult to get customers to recognise the validity of such investment calculations – low price in relation to high effect. However the arguments are like water off a duck's back. Price sensitivity is overshadowed by more important considerations: uncertainty, preferences for systems purchases, fear of making mistakes and cultural barriers.

Requirement differences: markets characterised by clear and considerable requirement differences often go hand in hand with the presence of differentiated and focused competitor strategies. In reality this reduces the chance of success for a new business venture if its unique offer is tailored to the same pattern.

Resource and competency requirements

Entrepreneurs have scarce resources at their disposal and possess fewer competencies than large-scale, well established companies. Consequently it is smart to look for a business definition that can be realised with a sharp, narrow core competency rather than a battle fought in the field of resource quantity. A business definition based on knowledge resources rather than physical brawn, customised to fit segments with relatively low entry barriers and concentrating on very specific value fields will – all other things being equal – have the best chance of succeeding.

Cost relations

Some markets are difficult to attack for a start-up enterprise as a consequence of cost ratios. If high volumes lead to lower costs as a result of economies of experience and scale, it may prove impossible to gain a profitable foothold – even though a market could be created by means of a business redefinition. In such situations it may be necessary to compromise via a sub-supplier strategy in which the entrepreneur enters into an alliance with his competitors and/or customers and sacrifices his own visibility for the sake of having a share of the economies of experience and volume.

116

4.6 Inventory: Creation of the business concept – in search of uniqueness

Below, the frame of reference that we have just presented has been translated into a question/hypothesis battery. By confronting the specific entrepreneurial project, business concept or corporate venture with the question battery it becomes possible to test the strength of its unique elements.

The question battery forces you to make up your mind about the unique elements of a business concept, the unique selling propositions which are impossible for the customer to resist.

No special type of interpretation is called for, but critical analysis and constructive discussion are intended. In some cases some of the subjects will seem irrelevant and can be disregarded.

DESCRIBE THE BUSINESS CONCEPT AND ITS UNIQUE OFFER:		AGREE	DISAGREE	?	COMMENTS
I	*The business concept I have arrived at is definitely unique because:*				
A	I have discovered needs that no one has yet recognised				
B	I have identified completely new needs that are emerging				
C	I have found a new way to differentiate				
D	The key is the ability to serve price sensitive customers				
E	The unique factor is the competency of the venture				
F	I have developed or am on my way to developing a superior product				
II	*In relation to the three basic dimensions, how is the business definition unique – in other words different/original compared to those already being marketed*				

A	I define the business on the basis of a narrow, clearly delineated customer segment				
B	The concept is aimed at a broad spectrum of all customer segments				
C	I envisage an entirely new segment				
D	I go for one single customer function among many				
E	My business definition is functionally broad				
F	I focus on entirely new customer functions				
G	I have developed a new and different technology				
H	The project has on a broad technology base				
I	The technology is extremely focused, and I do one thing better than anybody else				
J	I think that more is better				
III	**My strategic approach leads to a innovative, unique business definition because:**				
A	The enterprise will differentiate itself from the competitors in one or more of the basic dimensions				
B	The enterprise will differentiate its offer to customers to meet very different needs out in the market				
C	The strategy consists in focus, focus and more focus on specific customers, customer functions or technologies				

		Customer groups	Customer functions	Technology	
D	The market is growing explosively. We are doing the same as everyone else; there is no reason for differentiation				
IV	**I am going to put together a uniquely innovative business definition, because the market is developing:**				
A	The field of innovation will diffuse – new customer segments will be added				
B	The trend is in the direction of system purchases				
C	A technological substitution is knocking on the door.				
V	**My strategy for business redefinition in comparison to conventional ideas is:**				

	Customer groups	Customer functions	Technology
1	Same	Same	Different
2	Same	Different	Same
3	Different	Same	Same
4	Same	Different	Different
5	Different	Different	Same
6	Different	Same	Different
7	Different	Different	Different

VI	**What is really" the secret" of my project idea/case? Business definition? Product definition? Specific competencies?**
VII	**What am I most uncertain about concerning the business definition? Does the viability of the idea depend on external factors that may or may not materialise?**

Testing the business concept in relation to market dimensions

The creation of the business concept does not take place in a clearly distinct process once and for all. Chapter 4 has looked at the fundamental dimensions that new as well as existing enterprises have to consider in order to ensure vital business definitions.

In practice there is a long way from the view permitted by the window of opportunity to the sustainable business concept. An irresistible offer to specific customers is the unambiguous, clear objective that any entrepreneur should be striving towards.

Literature

Abell Derek E. og Hammond J.S.: *Strategic Marketing Planning –Problems and Analytical Approaches.* Prentice Hall. 1979.

Abell Derek E.: *Defining the Business – the Starting Point of Strategic Planning.* Prentice Hall. 1980.

Levitt: Theodore: *Marketing Myopia.* Harvard Business Review 1960.

Nielsen Orla og Wilke Ricky: *Organisationers købsadfærd i grundtræk.* Samfundslitteratur. 1999.

Williamson Oliver: *The Economic Institutions of Capitalism – Firms, Markets, Relational Contracting.* Free Press. 1985.

5. Entry barriers to markets

> "Even a high tower starts on the ground."
>
> *Japanese proverb*

Entry barriers are obstacles and obstacles that have an impact on the chances of the enterprise to gain a foothold in the market – the first real condition for success. Entry barriers vary over time and across industries. Seemingly impenetrable barriers may crumble if conditions suddenly and unpredictably change. Barriers have not necessarily been raised as a protection against new ventures – but may be inherent to an industry or a cluster of enterprises.

The efficiency of a barrier as a hurdle will depend on the new business concept. Entry barriers cannot always be observed or charted like overseas mountain ranges. They hide and accessibility requires exploration, imagination and special equipment.

This chapter identifies situations with particularly high entry barriers and introduces the top indicators that will reveal the likely strength and direction of the competitors' responses to new ventures. Furthermore, the chapter subdivides entry barriers into two main categories: the incumbents' (a) cost protection, and (b) quality advantages. Both types of barriers will become evident in the form of problems in achieving customer acceptance of the new venture. In addition to this, we look at four unconventional strategies for forcing an entry across the barriers: The Trojan Horse, On the Back of a Tiger, the Movable Target and Jack the Dullard.

The conclusion is that entry barriers are like two-edged swords. At the same time a threat and an opportunity. It entirely depends on the business idea.

5.1 Introduction to entry barriers

An entry barrier is – to put it simply – an obstacle or hurdle that you as an entrepreneur meet and must either beat, get around or reduce through an irresistible business idea. The driving forces of industries are dynamic; they are influenced from many sides and keep changing form, direction and strength.

121

Seen from the point of view of the new venture, they constitute central risks, but they can also include fruitful roads to exploiting one's own competencies or to catching sight of opportunities others may have overlooked.

Market innovative and *technologically innovative* projects typically attack the challenge concerning entry barriers in different ways. Technologically innovative entrepreneurs tend to regard internal product development challenges as a greater barrier than the external entry barriers – customers and competitors. Underestimation of the external barriers is rooted in a natural faith in the product and the indubitable development potential of the venture. Particularly if a market is new, apparently without competition and with a product whose utility must be obvious to customers, it may be very difficult to imagine insurmountable barriers on the way to market penetration. In the unknown or unclear market situation the analysis of entry barriers is particularly difficult because uncertainty is high.

In mature industries with visible competition, established positions and well described buyer behaviour an analysis of entry barriers seems far more necessary and logical, just as certainty is higher. In principle the possibilities for successful new establishment should be noticeably smaller in hyper-competitive, saturated markets than in new industries in which positions have not yet been occupied. Nevertheless, the creative, knowledgeable entrepreneur has a chance of overcoming the entry barriers even in old industries by means of the launching of a new, customer-driven value formula. A new kind of business logic. That is how JYSK got started in an industry you would certainly have thought to be effectively closed to entrepreneurship.

Howdy Doody, my name is Lars Larsen

"My idea is the simple one of selling quality at slightly lower prices than my competitors", *Lars Larsen (1979) founder of JYSK!*

When you come to a JYSK store, there is always a bargain. From the start purchasing power and expansion were the key words – and they were to benefit customers. And by these means, JYSK succeeded in creating a culture entirely its own which has been the pillar of the company's successes over the years; straightforward, simple and down-to-earth.

The product and the customer were to be the centres of attention. In a plain and simple manner without any sophisticated frills.

During the 25 years since then, JYSK has grown into an international company with an annual turnover of more than €1 billion and more than 6000 employees. In 2003 the company had around 1000 shops all over Europe and in Canada – a total of 18 countries.

JYSK is a capital chain based on discount trade that attacked a market in which the players of the time were mainly quality orientated, weakly organised, specialist shops (duvets, eiderdowns, bed linen), not backed by any strong chain concepts. Larsen knew that purchasing power, and so scale, as well as cost management and positioning were the principal success factors of the industry. JYSK managed to gain a crucial lead by means of successful expansion.

Entry barriers can be subdivided into the following categories:

A. *Customer access*: what barriers are to be surmounted to get access to customers?
B. *Customer acceptance*: what fundamental factors have to be observed to achieve customer acceptance?
C. *Competitor reaction*: what countermoves can the competitors be expected to make?

Structural factors shape the underlying operational forces behind the actions and positions of strength of customers, channels and competitors, which form a barricade against new business entrants. External influences – suppliers, substitutes, complementary industries, etc.- will typically also play decisive roles. Nevertheless it is safe to say that these influences will be transmitted to an industry precisely by affecting customers, channels and competitors and will leave behind structures and patterns of behaviour among them which in turn, will act as practical obstacles preventing the entrepreneurial venture from gaining a foothold.

All the three barriers have to be considered although they do not necessarily have the same importance in all situations.

5.2 Entry barriers type A: Customer access

Without customer access there is no business.

It may sound absurd that a new idea that customers would really welcome may run into insurmountable difficulties in gaining qualified access to the market, to these very customers. In real life, however, such situations are quite common; the most suitable or the necessary channels reject innovation and, consequently, prevent exposure as well as volume. The reluctance of channels is not only caused by the uncertainty which always surrounds a newly started enterprise: will it survive? Will the idea catch on? How are the other suppliers going to react? Will the new product cannibalise the existing business of the channel? How serious is the risk? Will a small, new enterprise have sufficient resources to support commercialisation seen from the point of view of the channel? What about service?

Furthermore, a small number of factors can be identified – entrepreneurial situations if you will – in which customer access is associated with extraordinarily high barriers, see table 5.1. These situations are encountered especially in technological industrial environments – IT, for instance.

Entrepreneurial situation:	**Entry barriers:**
I. Global market while the window of opportunity is only open for a short time	*Time: Instant internationalisation* Access to effective international customer access/distribution from day one
II. Vertically integrated industry Channels are main competitors too	*Independence: No independent channels* Cannibalisation blocks third-party products
III. Distribution is in charge and at the same time views its role in the chain of supply logistically	*Price: Capital requirements for channel access* Capital requirements to minimise the risk to the channel/create return on investment
IV. Suppliers are in charge Biggest suppliers may threaten the channel with a ban on supplies	*Power: Threats of reprisals* Making the channel reject the innovation
V. The Good King The biggest and best channels offer partner programmes, visibility and joint campaigns	*The Image Trap: No commitment and real motivation on the part of partners to win through*

Table 5.1 Customer access – situations with extraordinarily high entry barriers

124

Time-to-market[33] is of decisive importance in a growing number of industries and value chains; lifecycle becomes shorter. Too late and too slow diffusion means that the train has already left when you reach the platform. If, conversely, you are premature, your liquidity will drain away before the market has even arisen. This is not only true of new entrepreneurial business, but new business is particularly vulnerable because, very often, it only has this one chance and does not have the financial resources for a second attempt. Access to customers – the right customers – in the first attempt is a matter of life and death.

If a market is global and the window of opportunity is open for a short time only, and if the channel structure is relatively fragmented – this is true of virtually all of the software market – access to end customers at the global level from day one is the most critical success factor. The newly started enterprise is handicapped in relation to incumbents who already have access to an international distribution network. Since it takes time to build sales and service channels, and because time is so crucial in relation to demand and production cycles, the entrepreneur is facing an extraordinarily high entry barrier.

The same is true if the degree of vertical integration is very high, which means that the production and the sales link are within the same financial sphere of interest – the global solution supplier with his own consultants, developers, platforms, applications, tools and hardware.

David and Goliath in groceries

New small enterprises that have developed exciting, appealing, fast moving consumer goods often run into a wall of insurmountable opposition from the distributors – the supermarket chains.

Not so much because retailers reject the viability of such ideas in themselves, or because they misunderstand the preferences of consumers and their wish for new things, but for the reason that, unsurprisingly, the chains wish to optimise the profit contribution of each space unit in the store. Existing products and brands will have to be removed from the shelves to make room for the new. Although circumstances differ from one country to the other, the basic pattern is the same everywhere: each supplier must take on the responsibility for creating a demand for their product range among consumers through mass communi-

---

33 Time-to-market: the speed at which an enterprise can introduce a product on the market compared to its competitors and in relation to the market's development.

cation, promotion activities, etc. In this respect the retail trade defines its role logistically; it provides room on the shelves on competitive terms and considers suppliers to be responsible for the market stimuli.

The capital requirements for achieving efficient distribution access for new brands in the international groceries market makes it virtually impossible for new, financially weak enterprises to get a foot in the door – entry barriers are insurmountable.

The image trap belongs to the more exotic and curious entry barriers. New enterprises often look for recognition, visibility, approval and acceptance by allying themselves to the leading suppliers in the industry. On the other hand, these often have a differentiated array of partnership programmes with varying contents and benefits that are offered to innovative small firms, which leaves the big company with a completely impenetrable palisade vis-à-vis its own customers.

It may seem farfetched to describe this type of relationship as an entry barrier, because the intention is quite the opposite. However, it often turns out that entrepreneurial enterprises attribute too much importance to such display windows; they fall into an image trap and confuse visibility with the generation of new orders and a communications medium with channels of acquisition.

5.3 Entry barriers type B: Customer acceptance

Customer access is a necessary, but not always sufficient condition for conquering market shares. Customer acceptance – from opportunity to congregation – is, of course, a correspondingly crucial entry criterion, and so it is also a tripwire.

Fundamentally, resistance on the part of the customer has to do with what forces are active in the specific situation, and the way in which they impact on customers' perceptions, considerations and buying decisions. Consequently, these forces also explain the incumbents' positions of strength – acting in the same way as protective barriers against outside threats. Accordingly, customer acceptance must be seen in a relative and often complicated format in which the competitors' positions as perceived by the customers play a crucial role.

Some common entrepreneurial views: Our offer to the market is unique; there is no direct competition on the horizon – what could go wrong? Or: Yes, we do have competitors, but our concept is many times better on the critical parameters. Or: Our technology is pioneering and represents a radical shift. All our competitors are tied down by old-fashioned thinking.

In reality competitors are generally fairly efficient opponents in the battle for customer acceptance. Logically you should not underestimate performance, functional and design attributes, production costs and hence price because they are important acceptance promoting elements. In some industries a new technology or a new application with better properties than the ones existing in the market may break through in record time, because the customers themselves are supplied with crucial new competitiveness for which reason they are willing to set aside all other considerations, in particular if timing is key. But far too often new business ventures die in infancy despite the fact that the solutions they embody would objectively lead to better need satisfaction than the existing ones, and all because other entry criteria influence the buying decision

Customer acceptance can be related to one of two dimensions, viz. the perceived relative price and the perceived relative quality. Graphically this can be shown as in figure 5.1:

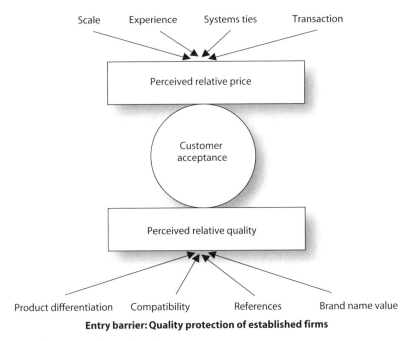

Figure 5.1 Overview of entry barriers to customer acceptance

Cost disadvantages are synonymous with insufficient price competitiveness. As an entrepreneur you should, therefore, always ask the following question: What are and how high are the cost advantages in the hands of the incumbents of the industry? What is required to neutralise or compensate for these advantages? These advantages do not necessarily hit you in the eye, but they are still there in a hidden form and will affect the customers' buying behaviour.

The concept "perceived relative price" should be understood in the broadest sense. The price is the total, perceived opportunity cost which a customer is facing when replacing his present supplier or changing established solutions thus taking on an unnecessary risk. The real calculation in decision making centres entails many such cost items and inertias. The following is a presentation of the barriers shown in Figure 5.1:

Economies of scale

Economies of scale reflect the diminishing unit cost as a function of volume per time unit. Large scale operations protect against invaders who will, initially, be short of volume. The existence of economies of scale faces new business ventures with considerable capital requirements that they can rarely meet.

Economies of scale can be located in all functional fields: development, procurement, production, sales, distribution, service, administration, management. As a rule, economies of scale constitute a major stumbling block for entrepreneurial ventures.

The cleaning industry and ISS

Traditionally cleaning has been seen as an industry with low entry barriers (anyone would have the wits to start a cleaning business) and through history it has been characterised by many, small, local firms with a high replacement cycle.

100 years ago, the ISS corporation was founded as a small Danish security company which later expanded by taking on board cleaning. Since then, ISS has managed to industrialise cleaning by creating economies of scale across all functions. Cleaning is a labour intensive process. Nevertheless, ISS has successfully managed to acquire economies of scale which no new start-up cleaning company could hope to match today.

ISS defines itself as a facility management partner and offers a broad spectrum of services: catering, building maintenance, property services, etc. – lines which ISS has been able to enter as a result of its cost position created by the company's ability to force through economies of scale in cleaning.

Industries with considerable economies of scale based on capital intensity will occasionally get out of equilibrium and will force down what are normally prohibitively high entry barriers, making room for entrepreneurial ventures. In situations with overcapacity, incumbent suppliers will for example defend their cost positions by making their capacity available to others, thereby effectively inviting competitors to enter the industry. It may be an appropriate decision to protect cost positions against other existing suppliers with a similar cost structure. But the risk of long-term confusion and erosion of the industry's total earning capacity seems obvious.

The story of Telmore

Operators of GSM mobile telephone networks wish to optimise utilisation of their network capacity to secure a high return on their investment and, with it, their cost position. At the same time mobile network operators (in Denmark) are under a legal obligation to make their networks available to others. The existing operators' own commercial stimulation of the mobile market was insufficient, or else the network capacity of the industry was fundamentally too big in relation to the demand. Under those circumstances the most important Danish operators – Sonofon and TDC – decided to sell net capacity on favourable wholesale terms to service providers who would lease their way onto the network and on that basis launch concepts and business models in direct competition with the net operators themselves. And that is how Telmore was created.

Telmore in Denmark concluded a net agreement with TDC Mobile and chose a simple, uncompromising strategy which, in its first phase, targeted young people: no subsidies in connection with the purchase of the mobile phone. Transparent prices for telephones, and text messages at low prices. Sales and service only over the Internet. Telmore – no nonsense, no frills. Competition in the Danish mobile telephony market for private users was very much centred on the acquisition of subscribers, and for this reason the suppliers massively subsidised the price of mobile handsets. So a customer might choose TDC Mobil, buy a mobile phone at a fraction of the price if they would also become TDC Mobil subscribers. At the next moment, the consumer may cancel her subscription and become a Telmore customer and use the TDC network.

In 24 months, Telmore achieved a market share of nearly 20%, the same level as the market leaders Sonofon and TDC.

The imbalance of the industry (overcapacity) created by the wish to achieve economies of scale left room for new competitors whose objective was to conquer market shares from those suppliers who, in a weak, incautious moment had been motivated to open op the floodgates to the market.

Experience curve

Many industries are being protected by the experience curve, i.e. declining unit costs as a function of learning through the accumulated production during the overall life of the product class. Experience curve advantages constitute an effective price barrier which is rarely overcome by competing head-on. Who, for instance, would be capable of taking up the battle of the global passenger aircraft market with Airbus and Boeing? Or challenge the motor car industry?

With his Virgin Cola, Sir Richard Branson challenged Pepsi and Coca Cola, but only with modest success; the price to be paid for acquiring the top-of-the-mind position with the consumers would simply be prohibitive for Virgin. And without being dominant or second in the mindshare – no sale. Apart from that, Sir Richard has had a tremendous success with his business idea across all industries and markets: "Up against fat cats".

System ties

Very often goods and services are part of a system in the customer's organisation or pattern of preferences. The term system should be broadly understood. A customer's present supplier thus enjoys some protection – for example against entrepreneurial ventures. System ties are not just a matter of being able to guarantee interoperability and persistence (proprietary standards) and assure the customer that no unforeseen consequences, disruptions or other factors will happen to the existing routines. System ties also occur by way of workflows and procedures that have to be changed if new concepts are introduced.

Sometimes the rejection effect as a consequence of system ties is surprisingly strong and in many ways irrational. Even when innovations can be shown to yield a high and fast return they are often rejected out of hand.

In the field of software – applications, tools, middleware – many start-up enterprises will nearly always encounter resistance and despite the superior quality and profitability of their concept. The potential customers' perception of the costs of innovations is entirely different: We know what we have.

It requires major changes to introduce something new. What will happen if it has a negative impact somewhere else? We cannot afford experiments. In critical fields, we take no chances at all. We prefer dealing with someone we know is strong enough, someone we know will be in the market ten years from now, and who has a lot of references. Not invented here – therefore not interesting …

In short, entrepreneurs who wish to compete in markets with system ties will have to execute their strategies through business models that will allow them to avoid as much as possible an unpleasant collision with the barriers constituted by these kinds of switching costs.

Transaction costs

Buying processes are associated with transaction costs the size of which may be considerable. In the same way as system ties, transaction costs form part of the customer's profitability considerations; they are in real terms part of the price and so constitute a barrier to customer acceptance. Transaction costs consist of three different items, the three Cs: Contact, Contract and Control.[34] Existing suppliers with whom a customer is satisfied always enjoy a built-in cost advantage. In transaction terms, it is costly to abandon an existing business partner or market leader, unless they have exploited the protection or leadership to cut the cake too much to their own advantage seen from the point of view of the customer. Why? Because, by definition, transaction costs are higher in connection with a shift than they are for a rebuy.

This is not only true for entrepreneurs and their enterprises, but may have a specially blocking effect for a new enterprise that is disqualified out of hand because of its size and lack of references.

However, exceptions do exist.

Navicon and the Royal Danish Navy

Navicon is a small Danish consultancy firm which develops IT solutions for its customers on an hourly basis in project form.

At one point the Royal Danish Marine was facing investment in a renewal of the land-based radar surveillance system of the Danish maritime territory.

---

34 Hougaard and Bjerre (2002).

Procurements included software to transmit radar images in so-called real time from data points to surveillance centres. The Navy invited bids from the few, but very strong leading global suppliers of this type of software; they had strong positions in the financial sector where the demands for security, simultaneity and robustness are crucial.

In transactional terms it would be a relatively simple matter for the Navy to choose the best or cheapest bid. However, the Navy chose to offer the job to the newcomer Navicon rather than procuring a well documented, globally leading solution. In the compromise between price and transaction costs, the Navy preferred a low price and high transaction costs.

The Royal Danish Navy wished for co-ownership of the new technology and saw itself as a professional partner in development and, therefore – for strategic reasons – preferred a transaction with an inherent higher risk.

The conclusion is that the perceived, relative price in terms of business economics represents an important entry barrier for customer acceptance. Economies of scale and experience curve occur visibly and are reflected by the price structure, the competitive environment and the level of profitability among existing suppliers. Barriers created by system ties and transaction costs may seem diffuse and occasionally irrational. They are, consequently, difficult to contain and circumnavigate.

Product differentiation

Product differentiation means that a supplier either differentiates his products in relation to those of his competitors or customises them to meet the needs of different market segments. Differentiation may entail a physical as well as a perception dimension, and in many industries it works as an effective blocking mechanism against entrepreneurial ventures.

How, for instance, is it possible to gain an entry into markets in which competition is massively concerned with conquering and managing perceived positions, that is to say, the customers' notions, and in which all possible positions have apparently been taken and fortified?

In industries with a high degree of product differentiation suppliers have apparently understood the value of effective segmentation and positioning. This, on the one hand, indicates the existence of relatively high entry barriers, on the other, it signals a market dynamism that may lead to market openings for new ventures.

Beer for the discerning palate

The beer market is characterised by keen competition, strongly fortified positions, not to say unconquerable positions for newcomer enterprises. Nevertheless, we do see successful examples of entry barrier penetration. Small and new breweries have managed to enter into co-operation agreements with big grocery chains, based on private labels, for instance in the form of discount products – that go into battle with the dominant brands. So-called micro breweries are another model at the other end of the scale. Beer is said to be capable of imparting the same flavour and taste experiences as wine; however, over the years these differences have become blurred and forgotten as a result of the industrialised supply offered to consumers in the shops over several generations. A supply with few and small flavour nuances, so that high-quality beer in terms of flavour has virtually ceased to exist.

Micro breweries produce beer rich in flavour in small quantities distributed through exclusive channels like beer-cafes. Their prospects are good. They have seen the demand among sophisticated consumers for an entirely different experience than the one offered by the common products.

Compatibility

Compatibility means that a supply or a product will seamlessly fit into a customer's activities and processes. Compatibility is not only a risk factor (and hence a cost) but also influences quality perception, whether it is a matter of lifestyle or high-involvement in the consumer market or the procurement of company cars in industrial markets.

Companies having bought a specific ERP system will prefer special applications from the same supplier to those offered by specialist suppliers. Even if these argue that they can deliver seamless adaptation and integration, the customers often choose the "second best" product with guaranteed compatibility.

References

At the basic level, lack of references may be an insurmountable entry barrier. Where experience curve effects leads to cost barriers references constitute an effective quality protection in the sense that customers perceive references as a quality stamp. In some cases, customers focus on references in their specific field, in other contexts the overall list of references of the supplier in question is assessed.

Lack of references may lead to venture failure. Despite an innovative approach and, possibly, a better solution for the customer he or she will often go for safety, which is tantamount to going for the recognised product.

There is no simple recipe for neutralising competitors' references. The newcomer enterprise may attempt to concentrate its foothold-gaining strategy on customers who are especially willing to run a risk, or who have done well by being innovators. Or they may try to interest customers in a joint venture development (pilot projects) in which the customer becomes the co-owner of the innovation and has a certain ability to influence things at a modest price and without any subsequent supplier dependence as competencies are internalised into the process.

Often newcomer enterprises can successfully position themselves far back in the value chain which might enable them to avoid the reference confrontation. For instance, by concluding OEM (original equipment manufacturers) agreements with big reference-strong players, who agree to acquire the innovation and often also to co-ownership or some kind of exclusive rights. The OEM partner's references become the snow plough of the entrepreneurial enterprise. In later phases, the young enterprise uses the end-customer references acquired as its own, and in this way buys customer acceptance for itself.

Brand equity

In many industries – for example, project orientated ones – references make up the very core of the brand equity.

Brand equity, understood as perceived quality, mindshare, loyalty and associations evoked[35] may represent a serious obstacle for an entrepreneur. Markets in which branded goods or corporate branding are predominant decision criteria for customers indicate considerable differences in customers' quality perceptions.

These quality differences detected and the perceived quality as such can rarely be eradicated by means of pure product development, not even if the properties of the new product are demonstrably superior. Brands occupy specific positions in the minds of customers, and this, in turn, governs their buying process.

---

35 Aaker (1991).

134

In principle it can be claimed that industrial procurement processes are based on rationality, and that brand equity in the consumer sense is a kind of disruption that should not occur. However, in practice it is not this kind of brand-neutral objectivity that an entrepreneur encounters.

Dog Farts and Seagull Droppings

In 1985, when Michael Spangsberg bought the slumbering company Bon Bon, the Danish market for licorice (Denmark is the world's biggest consumer of salt licorice) was dominated by well known brands like Pingvin, Haribo and Lagerman.

Spangsberg, who had a history in the biscuit industry, thought that BonBon had an unredeemed potential if new packaging could be developed – big bags for supermarkets, new flavours and, last but not least, appeal directly to the customer segment children. As Spangsberg puts it, kids like to try new things, preferably something that is boundary-transgressive.

By means of brand names like Dog Farts and Seagull Droppings, Bon Bon managed to realise the notion of reaching the target group children via boundary transgression – adult outrage – with a hint of humour and vulgarity.

Retailers were fairly categorically in their rejection of the new Bon Bon concept until a series of television commercials about real dog farts were a major hit in 1989. They created a magnetic effect which really did force the retail trade to include Bon Bon products in their range.'…

Then things went forward quickly and Bon Bon sped up product development through entirely new flavour combinations – salt licorce and fruit gum, but also completely new exotic flavour dimensions in hard candy.

Before the competitors had time to react, Bon Bon had managed to conquer 12% of the Danish small-bag candy market. By way of a side benefit, the entertainment park Bon Bon Land was established, which by now is frequented by 500 000 people every year.

In addition to this, Bon Bon started exporting to Sweden and Norway as well as Continental Europe – with mixed results; consumers' perception of licorice differs widely in geographical terms.

Bon Bon successfully thought out and implemented its positioning strategy which benefited from the values – or rather counter-values – of kids.

Entry barriers are not necessarily static and uniform for all. The unique offer represented by an innovation will sometimes be able to influence entry barriers positively. For instance, because the innovation represents a complete break with existing habits. It would be completely unthinkable for wind turbine energy to compete with other types of electricity generation on market conditions.

If wind energy has nevertheless become as prevalent as it has, it is due exclusively to public subsidies and other types of incentives leading to an artificial reduction of entry barriers. The wind turbine industry itself is the originator of its own success. By being able to present the technology and solutions backed by a convincing profitability calculation, the industry has been able to move political systems in the direction of wind and, has been able to lower the entry barriers enough to make it possible to achieve a considerable market.

5.4 Entry barriers type C: Competitor reaction

In addition to customer access and customer acceptance, competitor retaliation is obviously a barrier that the entrepreneur will always have to consider. The intention, substance and direction of countermoves generally will depend on an unbiased assessment among incumbent suppliers.

Correspondingly it is important for the entrepreneur to understand what kind of countermoves may be expected, from whom and why so that to the highest possible degree the project can avoid destructive countermoves. Great uncertainty will always be associated with this and, logically, the entrepreneur will normally concentrate most of his attention on customers and channels rather than competitors.

The patterns of reaction will normally vary depending on factors like the nature, maturity, capacity utilisation and level of satisfaction among incumbents. Similarly the number of competitors will normally also play a crucial role. In situations with relatively few suppliers they will often find each other in an agreement about unwritten rules such as reasonable prices, relationship with suppliers and patterns of influence in relation to substitutes and potential invaders.

Some territory dominant market leaders are fully aware of newcomers and are willing to pay a very high price to prevent newcomers from gaining a foothold. Other market leaders react slowly or smugly being fully convinced of their own strength when it comes to the crunch.

As a general rule, the big players in an industry tend to view the other big ones as more of a threat than small entrepreneurial ventures. They may even consider it an advantage that there is a small underbrush of new innovative enterprises whose role will be to test the new concepts and business models. If they develop successfully, the young firms will be acquired. In the reverse situation the industry has saved itself costs, which turned out to be wasted.

Table 5.2 below contains a list of indicators for competitor counter-moves:

What indicates a strong and quick reaction?	What indicates a weak and slow reaction?
• *History* History shows that new players get rough treatment in the market	• *Assumptions* Competitors are ill informed. Or they do not notice what is happening
• *Resources* Incumbents have very considerable resources at their disposal	• *Calculation* It is not worthwhile for incumbents to quell the venture – for example due to customer inertia foreseen
• *Strategic obligations* Incumbents are entirely dependent on the industry and have high non-liquid investments	• *Cannibalisation* They find it difficult to act concretely, for instance, because it would cannibalise their own business
• *Growth* The industry is growing more slowly or is in decline	• *Conflict* They have mixed motives and conflicting objectives
• *Visibility* It is necessary to send an unambiguous signal to existing competitors	• *Unclear positions* Competitive behaviour in the industry leaves doubt as to who should react to invaders
• *Head-on attack* The leader(s) exposed to a head-on attack	• *Niche* The new enterprise concentrates on a niche that the incumbents have either overlooked or consider uninteresting

Table 5.2 Top indicators for competitor reactions to a new business venture

If competitors' reaction do not materialise, this can either be good or bad news.

Flying enterprise

Enterprise was established in 1957 by Jack Taylor, and today his son Andy is in charge of the company. Enterprise has grown to become the biggest US car-rental company with a fleet of over 500,000 motor cars and 50,000 employees. Car renting is a mature and very competitive industry with two dominant suppliers, Avis and Hertz, which have a history indicating that alertness and focus on good service provision. Nevertheless, Enterprise has managed to become a shining success.

Enterprise chose to focus on a niche which their competitors – which at the time were much bigger – ignored, i.e. letting loaner cars to customer who had been in an accident or whose engine had broken down or who simply needed a car while their own car was at the workshop.

This market is far more difficult to service than the airport market where customers place their orders in advance. The replacement car market is unpredictable, and demand varies strongly from one day to the next. While the car rental industry is traditionally heavily hierarchical and concept orientated, Enterprise has chosen a high degree of decentralisation combined with a strongly value-based type of management and an almost exaggerated focus on customer satisfaction.

Today Enterprise asks customers two, but only two, questions: "Were you satisfied with our service?" And, "Are you coming back to us?"

Enterprise avoided a head-on attack on Hertz and Avis and instead chose to concentrate on a niche which the two market leaders would not or could not specialise in – apparently because their pre-conditions in terms of corporate culture was different.

5.5 Unconventional roads to the market

For a small, young enterprise wishing to enter an existing market in which the most interesting positions are already occupied, entry barriers are very reminiscent of a vertical mountain wall or a high tower at the foot of which the entrepreneur stands. The situation is completely different in new product markets which nobody owns and in which the agile entrepreneur can win a valuable lead. Niche strategy can – as was the case for Enterprise – be a successful route across entry barriers in a start-up situation. Both since as a rule competitors are concerned about the most attractive segments and because focusing forces the entrepreneur to be very specific about what they will choose and what they will reject and about understanding their customers' needs.

The newly started enterprise is weak in terms of resources and can rarely afford a war of attrition or failed attempts at establishing (although Henry Ford went bankrupt three times before he had success.). That is why it is important to find a way into the market which minimises any risk of a fatal meeting with entry barriers. To put it more simply: it is a matter of circumnavigating the barriers protecting the incumbent suppliers of the industry.

Some unconventional methods could be:

- The Trojan Horse
- Riding a Tiger
- The Movable Target
- Jack the Dullard

The Trojan Horse

In Greek mythology, the Trojan Horse was a hollow wooden horse full of warriors that Ulysses tricked the Trojans into rolling into their city, after which these warriors attacked their opponents. The outnumbered attackers thereby avoided the unconquerable ramparts of Troy. Entrepreneurship par excellence. The Trojan Horse has to do with the art of disguise.

Honda and the others

The entry of Japanese brands onto the American motor car market was, of course, noted, but at the same time it was played down by the big – American – car manufacturers. At the time, the consumers virtually all wanted to drive big, well-equipped, imposing battleships – read: American cars. Product development and competition centred on this giant market whereas the demand for mini cars was considered to be fairly uninteresting.[36] When the first oil crisis left its deep tracks through our economy, consumers became far more interested in energy saving cars which, at the same time, was a signal of social consciousness.

The early, small Japanese cars proved to be Trojan Horses as they created a platform for climbing up the market so that the Japanese ended up being able to compete head-on in the luxury car market, the family car market and the mini car market. The success of the Japanese cars was facilitated by VW that, at the time, was dominant in the compact niche, but whose strategy was to climb upwards in the market. At the same time, the Japanese brought with them a quality and cost revolution and, in this way, forced the American manufacturers to look inward and create radical improvements.

This history was identical with that of the Japanese motorbikes in Europe, although without the oil crisis as a decisive impulse. First the Japanese went

---

36 D'Aveni (1995)): "While niching and outflanking competitors are not a tremendous threat to the full line producers at the outset, in the long run they can spread across the market like a forest fire, as was the case in the U.S. auto market. By establishing themselves in a small segment, they can move out to take over progressively larger portions of the market....".

for the 250 CC segment – first-time buyers, the youngsters. Then the 500 CC segment, when customers were about to replace the bike for a bigger model, etc.: by now, consumers had become accustomed to Honda, Kawasaki, Suzuki, Yamaha; they were well satisfied and loyal to the brand. Triumph, BSA, Norton and many others disappeared from the market in the course of a few years.

As previously mentioned a Trojan Horse may consist in a purely sub-supplier strategy in which the solution of the small enterprise is integrated as a module or component in an application or an end product – even though the long-term ambition is to become an application supplier themselves. Therefore, the motto is: "Move backwards in the value chain." Let the giants fight the war for the end customers. Strive to become embedded in the products/solutions of those established players that the young enterprise really sees as its future main competitors. Avoid competition. Not everyone needs a slogan like "Intel inside". For the small enterprise striving for competency development and strategic room for manoeuvre it is sufficiently ambitious to strive for a position as "inside Intel".

Many projects logically enough start with the dream or the idea about the end customer product, not about a component. Seen from a distance the entry barrier – customer access, for example – looks rather small.

Riding a Tiger

Someone who is – metaphorically – riding a tiger will have their strength doubled many times over giving them the chance to win. Riding a Tiger means that you define your business concept in the slipstream of the market leader and adjuste to the strategy of the leader.

Microsoft has been such a tiger. Application firms like for instance Navision, which has consistently been riding the Windows tiger has had immense success. The American advertising agencies, accountancy firms and consultancies rode the tiger which the globalisation of US enterprises in the post-war years created.

It is important to understand the nuances in the specific situation. To lean against an industrial standard may possibly remove an obstacle, but certainly does not guarantee success.

It is a necessary but not a sufficient condition that the tiger is within reach. Thus timing is of the essence. For instance, in practice it is impossible to jump on to the back of the tiger when it is moving at top speed. Secondly, it is important to identify the tigers of the future. In the infancy of PCs it was difficult to tell whether to back Apple or Microsoft. And who could anticipate that Nokia – at the time a conglomerate of the more diffuse type – a few years down the road would dominate the global mobile phone market with a market share of close to 40%.

The Movable Target

Hit them where they ain't.

It may be exceedingly difficult for a market leader to throttle invaders if they are constantly moving, for example, in relation to distribution channels, customer segments, media, etc. Newly started enterprises may benefit from being quick and volatile in changing its marketing mix and by acting in this way – like a guerrilla – protect themselves against the enormous stationary firepower of the big competitors.

Jack the Dullard

"FAR in the interior of the country lay an old baronial hall, and in it lived an old proprietor, who had two sons, which two young men thought themselves too clever by half. They wanted to go out and woo the King's daughter; for the maiden in question had publicly announced that she would choose for her husband that youth who could arrange his words best".

Thus begins the fairytale written by Hans Christian Andersen about Jack the Dullard who rode straight into the princess' parlour on the back of his goat with some mud and a dead crow … and won the princess' heart while the squire's two sons were sent on their way.

Jack the Dullard's entrepreneurial plan consisted in reconfiguration, a sort of counter-positioning – seagull droppings and dog farts. Or as in the slogan of the Volkswagen works when they launched the classic Beetle in the US market: the world's ugliest car.

The eagle has landed

Very few people have heard of Eddie Edwards. But who does not know Eddie the Eagle. Eddie the Eagle Edwards first and, so far, only ski jumper from Great Britain, represented Great Britain at the winter Olympics in Calgary in 1988 when he became world famous. His jump was only about half the length of the top jumpers and he fully lived up to the Olympic ideal about the importance of being to take part and not to win.

But television went wild with enthusiasm when Eddie the Eagle was about to jump, and the phrase, "the eagle has landed," in an undisguised ring of irony evoked enthusiasm and newspaper headlines all over the world. Tribute was paid to Eddie Edwards as an anti-hero – he became a brand.

Incidentally Eddie Edwards is the holder of the world record in stunt ski jumps with 10 cars and 6 busses.

5.6 Inventory: The barrier wheel

In figure 5.4 you will find a summary of some of the most important entry barriers, viz.: customer access, cost barriers, quality protection and competitors' countermoves. The barrier wheel is intended as an analytical inventory in which you can gain an overview of the entry barriers new ventures will encounter. Perhaps it will not be enough to develop one, and only one barrier profile. The composition of barriers will depend on the strategy in question. To the extent that many newly started enterprises are approaching the market, the barrier wheel can also be used for a competitor analysis.

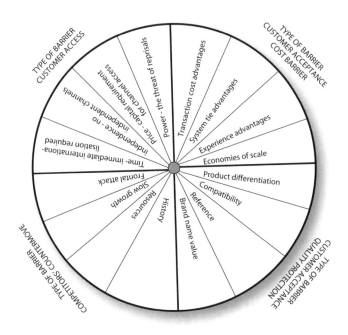

Scoring: High barrier: put a mark close to the circle. Low barrier: put a marker at or close to the centre.

The barrier wheel can both be used to uncover the importance of individual factors and to see which barriers one should watch and why.

As such the barrier wheel does not invite a quantitative interpretation. On the other hand you can make a direct reading of the scope of the difficulties that the new venture will encounter, symbolised by means of the barrier profile.

The message of Chapter 5 is that markets meet entrepreneurial ventures in different ways, and that different newly started enterprises are not welcomed in the same way. It can be quite difficult to simulate customer and competitors' reaction, but a typology of entry barriers can support an analysis. Rarely does an entrepreneur have the resources to overcome an entry barrier head-on whether it be a matter of channel access, communication, price wars, product development, etc. As an entrepreneur, you have to think smartly when it comes to entry barriers.

Literature

Aaker David: *Building strong Brands.* The Free Press. 1997.

Aaker David: *Managing Brand Equity: Capitalising on the Value of a Brand Name.* The Free Press. 1991.

Aaker David: *Strategic Market Management.* Wiley & Sons. N.Y. 1998.

D'Aveni Richard A: *Hypercompetitive Rivalries – Competition in Highly Dynamic Environments.* The Free Press. N.Y. USA. 1995.

Hougaard Søren, Bjerre Mogens: *Strategic Relationship Marketing.* Samfundslitteratur and Springer Verlag. 2002.

Porter Michael E.: *Competitive Advantage – Creating and Sustaining Superior Performance.* Free Press. N.Y. 1985.

Porter Michael E.: *Competitive Strategy.* Free Press. N.Y. 1981.

Times Jeff. A.: *New Venture Creation – Entrepreneurship for the 21.st Century.* Mc.Graw Hill. 1990.

Williamson Oliver: *Markets and Hierarchies, Analysis and Antitrust Implications.* Free Press. 1975.

6. Strategies for market entry

> "If you can look into the seeds of time,
> and say which grain will grow and which will not."
>
> *William Shakespeare, Macbeth, Act I, Scene III*

The moment when the newcomer entrepreneurial business meets the market is the moment of truth. Will we be accepted? Will customers hesitate? Will the business plan stand up? How will competitors react? Entrepreneurs have normally thought through their business concept very carefully and are very aware of the unique advantages their project holds for the customers. Nevertheless, it is a special task to translate the concept into an equally persuasive strategy for entry into the market. It is rarely possible to deduce the strategy automatically from the business definition; it normally requires separate considerations and decisions.

This chapter describes various types of environments and their impact on the choice of strategy for market entry. The chapter discusses how considerations of market attractiveness and core competencies can be combined. Similarly the chapter presents and exemplifies three strategic main roads to entry: first mover; differentiation; and generic product-market strategy. These roads reflect different conceptions of timing, sources of competitive advantages and competitor responses.

Many entrepreneurs uncritically take it for granted that the most obvious road to competitive advantages is to pursue the idea of being first on the market. One of the conclusions drawn in this chapter is that this doctrine can be a dangerous pitfall because it underestimates the efforts required to create a market; similarly it does not sufficiently answer the question of how to maintain and increase one's lead in a situation of competitive pressure.

6.1 Initial reflections on market entry

Many of the building blocks for successful market entry are formed during the phases in which the entrepreneur defines his market problem[37], relates to the window of opportunity, shapes his business concept and thinks through the interaction between entry barriers, the concept and competency. The strategy for market entry represents the essence of all these prior courses of events. Not as a passive projection, but as an independent proactive process in which the factors will have to be turned on their heads, taken apart and reassembled in new and creative ways again and again.

It is beneficial to look at the preparations for market entry of innovations as a search-and-learn process which takes place in close contact with customers, suppliers, distribution channels and other relevant stakeholders, a process in which the strategy is slowly crafted through destruction and rebuilding: searching, focusing, evaluating and deciding. And often it has to be done over and over. The arena of the three Graces (see Chapter 1).

Clearly enough, uncertainty will be particularly high if it is a matter of entering a market that does not exist and in which the innovation in itself constitutes the stimulus to create demand. From a distance, this situation in which the concept is new to the world looks like the dream start for a new enterprise, but is also a situation characterised by uncertainty, in which the rules are hazy and relatively impossible to calculate in advance. Therefore, in the early phases of establishment, it is important to form an impression of how much you actually know about the market and other factors pertaining to the environment.

The same is true of the degree of munificence or hostility of the market environment: What is the welcome that you may expect from customers and competitors going to be like?

---

37 Mullins (2003): "It is much more difficult to define the problem than the solution". Larry Keeley in Design Matters: "Basically innovation is all about a new surprising solution to a major challenge or a difficult problem ... If the answer is known in advance, the problem is not big enough".

When web-bureaus were born

When all of a sudden everybody needed to have a homepage of their own a new industry was born in record time – the web bureaus. The industry attracted thousands of start-up enterprises and led to the establishment of new business units in existing communication corporations. Market conditions were extremely attractive – growth rates explosive, customer access direct, acceptance unconditional, competitive pressure extremely low. In this market, there was simply room for everybody, and venture capital washed over the industry in ample quantities.

Far from all markets are as munificent. Industries with low growth rates, high investment costs, spare capacity, high price transparency and considerable buyer bargaining power are typically very hostile.

The nature of structural environmental factors creates the opportunities and restrictions within which a business venture in its start-up phase shall find its room for manoeuvre to introduce itself on the market. The room for manoeuvre can be described on the basis of the following distinction.

	Hostile environments	**Munificent environments**
Known market conditions	Attempt at prompt counter-moves, perhaps imitation / customers with strong bargaining power: 1. Cultivate a niche 2. Achieve effective differentiation	Immediate customer acceptance / growing market: 3. Always room for one more 4. Slightly better in one or several dimensions
Unknown market conditions	Sceptical or hesitant customers / pressured suppliers who will defend their ownership in the market: 5. Create new solution to an existing problem 6. Use existing solution for a new problem	Innovative customers / fragmented supplier structure: 7. Go for getting a lead 8. Look for partnership with customers

Table 6.1 Room for manoeuvre in establishment strategy in different market environments

Any enterprise, but particularly a start-up one, must always be on its toes – ready to adjust the strategy if the market responses so require. Consequently, the entry strategy *realised* ends up being a product of what is *intended and planned* in combination with what is *emerging*.[38]

Unknown market conditions make special requirements on the entrepreneur's ability to capture, disseminate and process information in the organisation, in the team. The reactions of customers and competitors often seem illogical or difficult to interpret – or perhaps even worse: they do not materialise at all and leave the entrepreneur in the dark.

Table 6.1 depicts eight simple recipes, rules of thumb, or definitions of room for manoeuvre. They may be considered as guidelines that can be modified, nuanced and adjusted to fit the specific situation. The most important message is to pay attention to: firstly, that the degree of the market as regards munificence versus hostility fluctuates a great deal depending on how *satisfied* and successful the incumbent suppliers are, and how *experimenting* leading customers wish to be. Secondly, there is no final answer to what the rules of the game will turn out to be during the innovative course of development and market formation.

An angle akin to the entry barrier issue has to do with taking a decision about whether the entry strategy should primarily be anchored in the *attractiveness of a market* or in the *unique competencies* of the project. Although attractiveness and competencies are not each other's opposites in connection with the launching of a new enterprise, they often have completely different implications for the start-up phase. The venture that focuses on opportunities and that uses market attractiveness as its springboard considers timing to be crucial and believes that the be all and end all of the success of the idea is speed. Even though entrepreneurship that is based on special competencies will often focus on timing too, the process is primarily driven by confidence in the entrepreneur's own ability and, thus, signals a certain amount of arrogance vis-à-vis competitors, who might possibly be the first, but who are rarely the best.[39]

This trade off between strategic angles can be illustrated in the following way:

---

38 Mintzberg (1998).
39 Duus (1997), Prahalad and Hamel (1990).

	Competency of the venture		
		High	Low
Market attractiveness	High		
	Low		

Table 6.2 Market attractiveness or special competencies as determinants for entry strategy

Source: Inspired by Growth Share Matrix (General Electric).[40]

Table 6.2 corresponds to the SWOT analysis[41] in which market attractiveness symbolises OT, while competency represents SW. The drawback of the SWOT-method is that it rarely leads to new discoveries and does not reveal real dilemmas because it is used in a manner which is to superficial and descriptive.

Competencies should not be confused with the topical product supply in a certain market or from certain companies. Let us compare things to a tree: products are leaves – and competencies are roots. The tree (competitors) is far stronger than their momentary positions (leaves) being supplied. Competencies are rarely visible, but give the tree its strength and nourishment.

Choosing between the competency road and the attractiveness road can be difficult:

Projects or products in young IT companies

Many small knowledge-based enterprises in the software field are facing the trade off between the project method and the product method in terms of market introduction. Undoubtedly, the greatest long-term financial potential is to be found on the product road – licensing fees and royalties from the sale of standard software, if it is successful, of course. The project method means that the enterprise offers to develop solutions tailored to the needs of the customers as an external development partner for the end customer at a fixed price or at a price based on time consumption.

Consequently, the project method is seen as an intermediary station in an attempt to arrive at the product method. The project method calls for fewer resources than the product method, where you are in direct competition with

---

40 Ref. for example, Kotler (1980, 1988), Cravens (1994), Aaker (1998)
41 Strengths, Weaknesses, Opportunities, Threats.

established companies, and where you have to deliver a completely finished piece of software with documentation, support, etc. Furthermore, the product method calls for customer access through competent partners and efficient distributors often across national borders, something that is costly to set up and operate.

The project method can represent customer financed product development; it improves the reference level of the company and provides invaluable experience concerning integration, functionality, development processes, etc. Entry barriers to the project markets are much lower – and scalability correspondingly more difficult to obtain.

The project method is therefore a detour towards proper product launching – a necessary evil. At the same time there is no guarantee that, at the end of the day, you will have a complete standard product. The needs of the project customers might prove to lead to de-focusing because they are too different, just as corporate culture tends to move towards consultancy arrangements so that, in reality, the project road takes you away from a future as a supplier of standard products.

Very often the dilemma in a small, newly started software firm has to do with the trade off between potentials and risks as described in the above example, and there is no final answer. The project method forces enterprises to meet customer demands quickly, which is healthy in view of the risks entailed. Enterprises that have created very promising technologies and applications and which have been successful in attracting substantial venture capital will typically choose to take the direct road towards product launching. Here too the risk factors are obvious. Enterprises lock themselves into development euphoria, and only far too late do they get information of the needs and wishes of the customers. The management – the founder – who is usually techno-orientated, affects his surroundings with arguments to improve the product so that it can do even more before it is introduced on the market. Suggestions and ideas from future users are immediately used as an alibi for continuing development efforts. And the commercial functions that are finally being built up within the organisation become like foreign bodies without sufficient gravity.

Different theoretical descriptions exist concerning possible entry strategies.[42] The following sections will introduce and discuss a typology consisting of

---

42 Many typologies exist to describe entry strategies, e.g. "Aggressiveness versus focus for the entry strategy leading to four types of entry strategy: (1) The Blitzkrieg – aggressive, broad front using wide scope of geography and market. (2) The cavalry charge – aggressive and focused. (3) The strike force approach – non aggressive and focused.

three different strategies that are closely linked to the conception in marketing literature of the most important sources for developing long-term competitive advantages:

A. First mover – the notion that long-term success can best be achieved by being a pioneer
B. Differentiation – or how, as an innovator, you can force your way into an existing market by means of irresistible advantages
C. Generic product market strategy concentrated on positioning considerations in relation to segments, products and competitors.

The approaches are not by definition mutually exclusive, but there is a clear demarcation line as, by definition, the first mover attaches himself to future markets and the breakthrough as well as dissemination of innovations, while B and C primarily describe how an entrepreneur can best make an entry into an existing market.

6.2 Entry strategy type A: First mover – first, the biggest, best

The first-mover strategy is a classic, very popular among entrepreneurs and linked to some of the most admired personalities in business history. You will find it in the standard marketing and strategy literature as one of the most glorious and attractive roads to growth and market leadership. Studies[43] show that the majority of the world's leading brands were also among the

---

(4) Guerrilla tactics. Hills et alt. (1994) or D'Aveni (1995): (1) Superior stakeholder satisfaction, (2) Strategic soothsaying, (3) Speed, (4) Surprise, (5) Shifting the rules, (6) Signalling and (7) Simultaneously and sequential strategic thrusts.

43 Several studies show that being a first mover is worth while in the long run, A study of 500 mature, manufacturing companies in the PIMS database showed that first movers accounted for 30% while early followers accounted for 21%. A study of 18 consumer markets showed that the enterprises/brands that had been the first to establish themselves achieved a lasting market advantage. The PIMS database shows that the first-mover advantage is biggest in industries with high prices and relatively little product innovation as well as in markets where products provide high added value for the customers.

first ones to be introduced in their respective markets, and that probability seems to indicate that the frontrunner has also the best chances of long-term success.

From vitamins to Valium

To be the first to arrive in a market with an innovative product may prove to be an extremely powerful strategy. Hoffman-LaRoche was a small, ailing chemicals company until the time when the company took advantage of timing and a knowledge-based lead to make a quantum leap to become a worldwide pharmaceutical group. Hoffman-LaRoche grasped the opportunity and began producing and selling vitamins which, at the time, were not certified medicinal products. Later on, Hoffman-LaRoche was the first company in the market to introduce sulpha drugs and even later psychopharmacological drugs like Valium and Librium. Each of these strategic steps was the result of systematic first moving and turned out to be extremely successful.

The example of Hoffman-LaRoche emphasises that the crucial condition for a successful first-mover strategy is unique knowledge and competency rather than a sense of perfect timing in attractive markets.

The desirability of being a pioneer is obvious in many research and development based sectors in which there is competition for patents and scientific discoveries leading to proprietary rights. Whenever physical possibilities are crucial, whenever the winner takes it all, and where the uncertainty about the latent market seems to be minimal because of clearly recognised needs, and eager-to-buy customers, the first-mover-advantage is immediately clear.

However, such factors are not necessarily present in all industries. The first-mover strategy is one that is based on the idea that timing is everything, which, to be sure, is an eternal characteristic of all business acumen, but not necessarily tantamount to saying that first is best. To be the first to introduce more or new technology – irrespective of price – is not by definition identical with the best solution for the customer:

Niels Jacobsen, CEO, William Demant (Oticon) – European Company of the Year 2003

"Pipeline management calls for an extremely profound knowledge of the industry and good commercial flair and skill. By means of perfect timing we have been able to supply the market with new product families which have conquered market shares ... The businesslike approach to things, thinking like a businessman – is the essential element ... Sometimes we see that some of our competitors, because of the way in which they have organised themselves, attach more importance to technical feasibility in their decision making process than to what the market out there demands ... Some competitors focus on the technical aspects and talk about the hearing computer, etc. That is without any relevance for the end user ...".[44]

Optimal timing and technological leads are not synonymous concepts in the hearing aid business according to Niels Jacobsen, Oticon, which can present annual growth rates of more than 25%. This is a thought that many entrepreneurs need to get accustomed to, people whose innovative strengths are often more technical than businesslike.

Although the first-mover strategy was a classic in theory as well as practice, it was the Internet bubble from 1998-2000 which really linked the first-mover strategy and entrepreneurship together. First moving became the "Open, Sesame" of the new economy. In particular, e-commerce projects were supposed to entail front-runner advantages as their unique strategic argument. Their only advantage. In short: first, biggest, best.

First moving became the magic spell of that strangely wild epoch. As everybody knows today, consumers were much too hesitant in accepting the innovations and invitations of the new economy. Even in those markets where e-commerce did in fact achieve a considerable volume (the book market), first movers did not outclass the leading brands of the old economy, which swiftly found efficient countermoves. First moving did not lead to any protective position.

An illustrative example from the dotcom world:

---

44 The Danish daily, Børsen, 10 June, 2003.

Customer economy and e-commerce[45]

Although many e-commerce enterprises collect data about their websites, only very few knew how to interpret the data and, consequently, did not manage to become more efficient over time. As long as venture capitalists were willing to throw money at the dotcoms, profitability was not really important. Or was it?

An extensive survey carried out by McKinsey & Company in 1999 may shed some light on what really happened. At least six months prior to the definitive collapse of the dotcoms, data showed that the Internet companies were suffering from a fundamental delusion. They were successful in attracting unique visitors to their websites, but they bought virtually nothing, and very few buyers returned for more.

The survey included more than 650 million unique visitors at eight different websites who between them made 2.7 billion visits and effected 27 million transactions and paid $4 billion to 224 firms.

Data showed that less than 4.5% of the visitors actually made a purchase, and less than 10% of those who did return to buy later on. Later in the year, the percentage of buyers dropped to 2.5 of which 18% returned. During the first six months of 1999 it cost more than $1,100 to acquire a customer who, typically spent a little over $400 on at least two purchases during the period in question ....

In short, consumers were far more attracted to the experience than to the opportunity to buy. The first-mover advantage was, and remained, an illusion.

It could be asserted that the e-commerce example does not really prove anything about possible first-mover advantages because the problem was really the absence of demand on the part of customers; there was a lot of fascination, but no demand. If the Internet users of the world had started to trade massively over the Internet from day one, we might, hypothetically, have thought that first would also be biggest and best.

A first-mover strategy is worth while, first and foremost if it seems likely that entry barriers will grow considerably and quickly. For a new business venture, the first-mover strategy does not, consequently, entail a universal chance; but it is undoubtedly an opportunity in certain situations. Advantages and disadvantages can be summarised as follows:

---

45 McKinsey Quarterly 2001

External situations with first-mover advantages:	External situations with first-mover disadvantages:
Experience curve Steep experience curve: Unit costs drop dramatically as a function of accumulated production	*Market volatility* Needs, segments and competitive conditions will change radically once the market starts growing
Awareness Low price to achieve positioning and brand value compared to later arrivals. Build up of change-over costs	*First-mover costs* Costs for creating markets are high – in absolute figures and by way of risk. Others will benefit from first-mover investments
Distribution Access to /control with the best distribution channels	*Technological turbulence* Technologies other than the first ones will come to dominate
Monopolistic profit Slow or delayed competitors' reaction tempt monopolistic price fixing	*Declining development costs* Development costs decline. It will be cheaper for the next-comers to establish themselves
Suppliers' side Access to the best suppliers	*Suppliers and distributors* Their roles will change and their importance be reduced in step with the maturing of the market
Standard Opportunity to develop into becoming industry standard as a result of the size and composition of the customer base	*Market insight* Insight into the market increases and reduces the risk of wrong decisions

Table 6.3 Advantages and disadvantages of a first-mover strategy for a start-up enterprise

We should be wary of generalising across industries. To exchange the *short-term* first-mover advantage for *long-term* competitive advantages requires the new enterprise to have resources for an aggressive investment into the build-up of the market and to maintain the lead. The specific recipe for this varies, but may be summarised under the following headings:[46]

---

46 Aaker (1996).

A clear vision for the mass market[47]

It is usual and sensible for the first mover to focus on small, professional, innovative, product-enthusiastic, large-scale consuming customer groups on the basis of a skim-off-the-cream philosophy. Ampex was a pioneer in the video-recorder field, and for several years sold a small number of units at $50,000 until Sony and Matsushita seized on the idea of a mass market for videos and a price of $500. Timex had the same vision in watches. And Ford is probably the best example of the vision of a mass market in the industrial era.

Managerial perseverance

Even if new products originate in one or several technological breakthroughs it often takes many years of stubborn and targeted development efforts under uncertain conditions to create a market breakthrough. Try, for instance, to ask Mr. Finn Helmer who created Giga, one of the most fascinating enterprises in recent time, a man who had to spend many years in a relatively vain attempt to develop fast processors until the platforms of the enterprise fitted Intel to perfection. By acquiring Giga, Intel obtained fast access to a new market at a crucially important time.

Long-term financial brawn

Keeping up a long-term, capital intensive, deficit yielding developmental thrust at the expense of instant profitability does not simply call for managerial perseverance – it also requires financial brawn and patient, venturesome investors.

Unrelenting innovation

Long-term market leadership requires continuous, unrelenting innovation. It may seem tempting for a successful first mover to assume a somewhat conceited attitude, being completely convinced about the superiority of his own product. At some point, one's own product may start cannibalising existing business, which entails a risk that new products will not be launched, but postponed. In those circumstances there is a real risk of being acquired by the competition.

---

47 Also compare with Kim and Mauborgne (2000).

It follows from the above observations that the risks and disadvantages associated with first moving can be turned around and be seen as opportunities and advantages for ventures launched later on in the life cycle of the market. Therefore, it may be advantageous to introduce a new enterprise as an imitation or challenger. You avoid the pitfalls lurking for the pioneer: failed product development, high technological costs, etc. The distribution of roles, however, will typically be that new business ventures go for first moving, while incumbent enterprises postpone investment in a market until uncertainty about its emergence, size and structure has been considerably reduced. Best beats first.

Reversely, a *follower-imitator* strategy for market entry has a better chance of leading to success when the following conditions have been met:

- High accessibility – relatively low costs in connection with the acquisition of competencies including technological know-how
- The existence of a dominant design paradigm including de facto standards
- Possession of complementary assets allowing exploitation of the innovation

Whereas a first mover entrepreneur often has less strategic room for manoeuvre once the strategy has been fixed, the follower-imitator has a higher degree of freedom – everything from pure imitation, over modified imitation to capitalisation of brand values. Many of these second mover advantages can be collected under the heading of differentiation.

6.3 Entry strategy type B: Differentiation

First moving makes less immediate sense in a mature market. Here the innovative challenge to a newly started enterprise consists in finding relevant openings vis-à-vis the positions that the incumbents of the industry have already occupied and intend to defend.

Changes in or around a market, which will remove its equilibrium, will more often than not bring new entrepreneurial opportunities, but even static industries may occasionally be attractive because the incumbent suppliers have accepted their relative positions of strength just as customers have grown accustomed to the prevailing supply structure (also compare Chapter 2).

In the mature market, entry strategy has to do with efficient differentiation in relation to customers and/or competitors by means of a unique offer or a new and original approach.

A successful entry aimed at differentiation can be effected by exploiting one or more differentiation radials:

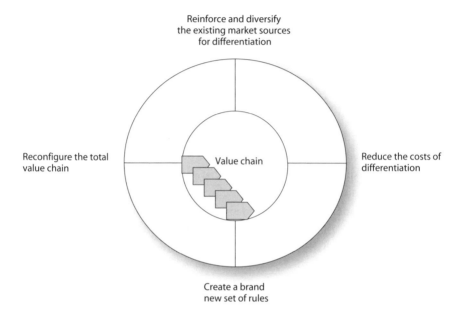

Figure 6.1 Differentiation radials for new ventures in mature industries
Source: Inspired by Abell (1979-1980)

The differentiation radials are both an integral part of the entrepreneur's creative market insight (also compare Chapter 2) and his ability to translate the discovery into a business concept.

Reinforce and strengthen the existing market sources of differentiation

Gaining an interest for new, innovative product concepts that will challenge customers' present selection buying behaviour may be an uphill strategy in the introductory phase. By contrast, it may be an advantage to capitalise on existing forms of differentiation by exploiting them even better.

Reinforcement of spreading to other parts of the value chain

It is claimed that Japanese car manufacturers carried out a comprehensive analysis of what Americans thought the "Beetle" did not have to make it the perfect mini car: accessories, comfort, roadability and handling. At the time the sources of differentiation in the car market plagued by the energy crisis were compactness, simplicity, and low operating costs. The Japanese understood this and were able to develop cars in the mini market that were better at meeting all these needs.

Increasingly, consumers in the western world are demanding convenience food – finished dishes that do not compromise high quality. Gastroprocess Technologies developed the voque at industrial scale and went into competition with batch frying, the only known processing mode known to the food industry. The voque process improves the tastiness while reducing process costs.

Whereas the convenience concepts of the established industry concentrated on storage and display in stores, distribution, an attractive range and good raw materials, Gastroprocess' differentiation spread to the processing phase itself.

Building bridges between customers' actual pattern of consumption and the intended use of the product

The perceived qualities and properties of a product will depend on the way customers use the product in practice, something that may differ substantially from the possibilities of the product and thus from the intentions of the supplier. In this way, a gap arises between planned and actual differentiation in which new venture opportunities are imbedded.

Full service mobile network operators offer their customers a broad selection of services. Qualities that can be used to justify a slightly higher price than those of the discount providers in the market. The problem is that the typical customer does not use these services often enough. As there is a positive correlation between how many services and applications customers use and their loyalty, telephone service providers endeavour to make them use the service while the new small service providers take advantage of the situation by signalling that from us you will pay for what you actually use – simple and transparent.

Exploitation of signals with a high perceived value reinforcing differentiation concerning essential selection criteria

A restaurant, for example, wishing to position itself as particularly gastronomic and hygienic, could throw open the kitchen so that customers could follow the preparation of dishes.

Skagen Food supplies freshly caught North Sea fish door-to-door all over the country. More than anything, the discerning consumer is looking for freshness when buying fish. In each package from Skagen Food there is a meticulous log of the specific fish: caught by which vessel; at which time of day; on which date; at what location.

To an entrepreneurial business the question is the following: How can the decisive selection criteria be better exploited and how do we do it?

Reduce differentiation costs

As a newly started enterprise you are free of the ties and traditions that are associated with the perception of the price for differentiation advantages. Strategically, entrepreneurs are more ready and do not have to fear inroads being made into their own business, they neither have to service a capital apparatus by way of fixed assets, nor are they tied to any particular image.

Thus, if differentiation is a source of competitive advantages, a cost advantage may arise through unconventional, untested methods.

Exploitation of differentiation advantages that cost nothing

As already described, differentiation can either be viewed in relation to competitors or practiced by creating unique benefits for different customer segments.

As a rule the latter form is a privilege for well established players with strong resources, while the chances for an entrepreneur are best served by developing advantages that cost nothing. This is an art mastered by the eccentric Chairman Simon Spies who succeeded in developing Spies Travel into a strong brand primarily by casting himself in the public arena getting a great deal of media attention for his stunts, happenings and, at times, rather extreme personal way of life, but also in direct opinion setting. The linkage of the brand and the individual Spies was unambiguous although it underwent transformation in step with trends in the travelling market.

Minimising the price for differentiation by managing the decisive cost generators

On the face of it, it may sound mysterious that new players may be able to introduce themselves by means of efficient differentiation that it has cost less to develop than it would have cost, for instance, the market leader whose bargaining strength, at least in theory, ought to be much higher.

Nevertheless, this road to the market is often very interesting even if the opposition looks invincible.

Budget airlines

The liberalisation of first the US and much later European aviation was the starting signal for the establishment of discount companies whose successes have surprised a lot of people and which make the local-flag-carriers – old symbols of national pride – look like wounded giants. In real terms, the discount carriers have managed to control a series of cost factors in a way that would have been extremely difficult for the traditional airlines to imitate. The most important of these factors are: a fleet of new aircraft – the most recent types of planes have a far better operating economy than the older ones; booking systems that entail minimal administration costs; lower airport charges because the discount companies avoid the costly, busy metropolitan airports (from Heathrow to Standstead); much lower wage bills avoiding the costly collective agreements; lower expectations on the part of customers, which means that the companies have introduced economies in the service field before, during and after flights.

Stressing differentiation where the newcomer enterprise has a clear cost advantage

Logically, the newly started enterprise, like everybody else, will emphasise the attributes leading to cost advantages that can be exploited as a relevant point of differentiation.

The stars from Morningstar

For a long time, the Danish market for analysis and rating of investment funds was a battle between a few national and fairly good suppliers. However, in 2001, Morningstar Denmark was founded as an affiliate of the worldwide corporation Morningstar. Because Morningstar is international, the organisation has at its disposal a detailed database covering investment funds all over the world. It is therefore possible to furnish customers with a rating method in which Danish funds are compared to corresponding funds globally and at the European level. This is not an option available to Morningstar's purely Danish competitors for whom it would be prohibitively costly to gain access to international databases. Thus, Morningstar has a differentiation advantage in terms of "international" rating at a price which is a tiny fraction of what this attribute would have cost the competitors.

Reduction of costs for activities of no value to buyers

If, seen from the point of view of customers, more is not better and if *more* comes at a price, and that is usually the case, an opportunity may arise to position the new venture, as the honest and transparent alternative to the incumbent suppliers.

This form of introduction may be a winner in industries in which competitors have gradually placed one layer after another of services and concepts for which not all customers will want to pay, something that is revealed immediately when the alternative appears. The retail discounter, Aldi is an excellent example of a company, which has eliminated everything in its shop layout and product display, which might be associated with price-increasing processes.

Create entirely new rules

Creative market insight will often make the entrepreneur discover new niches and so establish the foundations of a good business opportunity. New niches, new needs, new rules which will checkmate, or at least check, competitors.

Discovery of selection criteria nobody has seen so far

Book clubs

Fifty years ago when book clubs suddenly started mushrooming, this led to a substantial increase in the book market. It was not primarily the big publishing houses that launched the idea of book clubs, in which consumers would receive a number of book titles – only partly according to their own choice- against a fixed monthly payment. Entirely new customer segments, which had not previously bought novels or reference books, etc., were happy to join the new book clubs. What really happened?

At the time, a lot of single-family detached houses were being built. Homes were decorated with bookshelves as large groups of people had begun to take an interest in cultural matters including books; this was in the heyday of the Social-Democratic Party in which welfare and life-style aspirations were central to many people. The book? Well, the book was not primarily there for reading. It was supposed to be sitting on the shelf, looking good and sending out a signal of literacy. In short, new, and hitherto overlooked, selection criteria were at play. Books were chosen on the basis of the colour adorning their spines rather than their contents.

Book clubs are an example of new needs and new selection criteria that arose in connection with consumer behaviour.

Similarly, frequent flyer programmes, the world's most efficient loyalty programmes, have given rise to entirely new selection criteria and set new rules, i.e. the business traveller actually protects the interests of the supplier – the airlines – rather than those of his employer because he can reap personal benefits from doing so.

Affecting customer decision centres

Two of the above examples illustrate this type of differentiation in the establishment of a new venture. Microsound (hearing aids) wanted to sell through opticians' chains where consultancy is soft-core and style orientated rather than through hearing aid dispensers who are partly thinking in patient-treatment terms, and are partly influenced by the producer link. Microsound makes its stake on the end consumer being the real decision maker while being assisted by strong communication and counter positioning.

The method chosen by Bon Bon was to appeal robustly to a kids-versus-parents sentiment. Moving the centre of gravity in decision making away from the parents and over to the kid.

The strong trend towards self medication which, among other things, finds its expression in the explosively increasing supply of natural medicines and food supplements, also illustrates a shift in decision making from the doctor/chemist to the consumer herself.

Markets may get into disequilibrium if suppliers fail to react to changes in buying processes or preferences or if they do not even catch the signals.

Increasingly enterprises wish to postpone IT purchases. This has made software leasing popular. In this way and mainly for accountancy reasons customers can spread the actual purchase over several budgetary periods, something that is considered an advantage in times with tight liquidity. The software supplier who fails to be proactive in developing new financial models and packages will lose ground. And conversely: by means of alliances between financial institutions and software suppliers brand new trading conditions are being created.

Reconfigure the overall value chain

Sometimes innovations may lead to a complete change in the structure of the value chain. The invention of the container and the roll-on-roll-off concept changed everything in the transport market and the centre of gravity of capital charge. The company Fed-ex revolutionised the transport market for small parcels by acquiring its own fleet of aircraft thereby gaining control of the entire process flow from door to door, which brought down transport times considerably without adding any costs.

More than anything the dotcom epoch had to do with reconfiguration. For instance unrestricted future dominance was predicted for online auctions, virtual purchasing associations in which consumers join forces by unifying their purchasing power, virtual shopping malls and digital intermediaries acting as the customers' agent vis-à-vis suppliers without revealing the identities of customers, etc.

Michael Porter in 2001:[48]

"It is hard to come to any firm understanding of the impact of the Internet on business by looking at the results to date. But two broad conclusions can be drawn. First, many businesses active on the Internet are artificial business

---

48 Porter (2001).

competing by artificial means and propped up by capital that until recently had been readily available. Second, in periods of transition such as the one we have been going through, it often appears as if there are new rules of competition. But as market forces play out, as they are now, the old rules regain their currency. The creation of true economic value once again becomes the final arbiter of business success."

Although differentiation can squeeze ajar the doors of an existing market for a new enterprise there are also pitfalls into which it may fall. Some of the most frequent are:

1. At the end of the day the customers do not really appreciate the unique points
2. The degree of differentiation is too high and consequently is not accepted
3. The extra profit you are going for is too high in relation to the perceived quality
4. The enterprise ignores the benefits of signalling value
5. The enterprise is unaware of the costs involved in differentiation
6. Focus on product rather than to the value chain as a whole
7. Insufficient attention to the diversity of the segment

New products on industrial markets will normally encounter higher resistance among customers than might objectively seem justified: established solutions are chosen over machines based on new production methods with an indubitably high return on investment for the customers. Administrative software simplifying work flows and reducing costs and fully compatible with existing platforms still do not gain a foothold. New development methods, simulations, embedded solutions, etc., which can unquestionably cut development time for new products and reduce time-to-market without any negative side effects and the customers still will not buy them because they would require changes to the existing work flows.

All businesses have their particular cycle of renewal and specific mode of implementation: who will be the first to take on new ways of thinking? Through what channels do innovations flow – i.e. the sources of differentiation? What do the decision centres in the customers' organisations look like, and what do the decisive access criteria consist in? The risk that customers will not appreciate the unique aspects of differentiation can often be traced back to the traditions and innovation culture of the industry in question.

6.4 Entry strategy type C: Generic product-market strategy

In section 6.3, differentiation was described on the basis of the *substance* of the unique selling proposition with which the newly started enterprise intends to meet the market.

A somewhat different approach may be to view differentiation from a *positioning* point of view epitomised in the question: based on our knowledge of the customers, the positions of our competitors and our own competency, in which markets and with which offers will our chances of success be the best? How narrow/wide should introduction be and on what grounds? Figure 6.2 below outlines four different product/market strategies for the newly started enterprise:

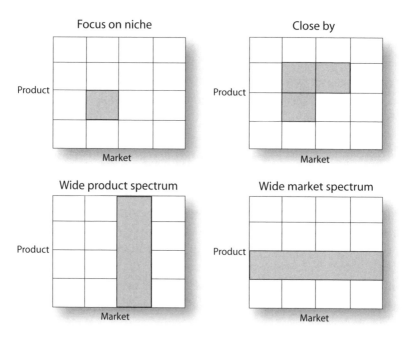

Figure 6.2 The four generic product-market strategies for the newly started enterprise

Behind all the four generic strategies you will find value chain based differentiation vis-à-vis the product-market matrix of the competitors. The choice between certain pure generic product-market strategies during the introductory phase will depend on:

- The attractiveness of the market.
- Segments: how significant are the requirement differences?
- What core competencies does the venture have in absolute and relative terms?
- The position and preparedness of competitors.
- Access criteria seen from the point of view of customers.
- Attitude to risk.

One entry road that many entrepreneurs would consider immediately attractive is *niche focusing*, i.e. focusing on one single customer group with a very specific offer. If the entrepreneur has a profound knowledge of the niche and a competency adjusted to the special needs and requirements of that particular segment, and is at the same time superior to his competitors, this focus might prove capable of blazing the trail to a successful entry. The disadvantage is that all the eggs are put into one basket, and if you misread the market or your own strength profile the consequences might be fatal.

Commodore, one of the very first products on the PC market, staked a lot on Commodore 64 with a joystick for kids – i.e. games and entertainment. However, this was not the niche to enjoy the first breakthrough.

The strategy *close-by* is a modified focus strategy: somewhat broader market focus with the possibility of a performance profile with wider coverage in terms of needs and requirements. The enterprise is thinking in somewhat more experimental terms, it is ready to learn and adjust if the primary target group should reject the concept, or if competitors try to prevent the entrant from gaining a foothold. A graphic depiction of this entry strategy, it might look something like this:

	Basic version	Advanced version
Specialist shop		X
Supermarkets	X	

Table 6.4 Close-by: modified niche strategy

One such example could be that the entrepreneur has developed a prototype of a brand new household appliance which carries out the same functions as existing products, but far more labour effective and with a higher utility rate.

The enterprise is uncertain about how best to make the product take, and therefore chooses a two-pronged introduction, one aimed at the broad consumer market through supermarkets, and another aimed at the more sophisticated, semi-professional specialist shops.

Digitarian

In early 2003 DVD players had really made it with a penetration of around 500,000 – 10% of all households in Denmark. Digitarian, a newly started company saw the possibility of renting DVD films to families with children exclusively over the Internet by way of a subscription scheme. You pay a fixed monthly amount and get three DVDs of your own choice which you may keep for a month. This business model meets the segment's need for saving valuable shopping time and money as the normal conditions in force in the video renting industry provide that the DVDs must be back within 24 hours.

The strength of Digitarian is, however, not the business model in itself, but the range of up to 3,000 titles to the distribution rights for which the enterprise had already secured in the specific channel within the concrete framework.

The above is a good example of a segment with a *wide production spectrum.*

The many virtual factory outlets that opened in the glorious days of e-commerce began on the basis of the idea of selling the most desirable designer clothes cheaply on the Internet. They were helping the labels rid their surpluses and yet did not succeed because the range that they had on offer did not have the requisite width, depth and topicality. Who can even remember Haburi, Gubi. com, Pets.com or Boo.com?

Attacking many markets simultaneously with one single product, that is applying the strategy to a *wide market spectrum* will, in many cases, require a disproportionate amount of resources unless sale problem is a simple one and the product does not require customising, etc.

Technologies with broad scopes of application, which are licensed to many application builders is another example in which market introduction takes place in an indirect and veiled form.

6.5 Inventory: Entry strategies

The checklist below summarises Chapter 6. You may, for example, use it as a sort of quality assurance for an existing entry strategy. Or you can use it as a source of inspiration for catching sight of the optimal angle in a specific situation.

Into what kind of market environment will the venture have to be introduced?

	I think the environment is hostile	I think the environment is munificent
Known market conditions		
Unknown market conditions		

Explanations and comments: _____

_____

_____

What is the point of departure for the venture?

		Competencies of the venture	
		High	Low
Market attractiveness	High	1	2
	Low	3	4

Explanations and comments: _____

_____

_____

		OBSERVATIONS/ COMMENTS
I	***External situations with first-mover advantages. Entry strategy has to do with first mover: which first-mover advantages can be achieved, and how do you circumnavigate disadvantages?***	
A	Experience curve Steep experience curve. Unit costs dropping significantly as a function of the accumulated production (not the same as economies of scale)	
B	Knowledge and loyalty Low price to achieve position and brand value compared to those entering later. Building up shift-over costs	
C	Distribution Access to/control over the best distribution channels	
D	Monopolistic profits Exclusivity in the markets tempts monopolistic price fixing	
E	Supplier side Access to the best suppliers	
II	***External situations with first-mover disadvantages***	
A	Standards Opportunity to develop into industry standard	
B	Market volatility Needs, segments and competitive conditions will change radically once the market starts growing	
C	Pioneering costs The costs of creating the market are high – in absolute terms and in the form of risk. Others will benefit from the pioneer's investment	
D	Technological turbulence	
E	Declining development costs Development costs will fall. It will be less costly for followers in the market to establish themselves	
F	Suppliers and distributors Their roles will change and their importance be reduced in step with the maturing of the market	

G	Market insight Insight into the market increases and reduces the risk of taking the wrong decisions	
III	**Opportunities in connection with differentiation.** **Reinforce and spread the markets' present sources of differentiation**	
A	By means of reinforcement or spreading to other parts of the value chain	
B	By closing the gap between the actual patterns of use in the industry and the intended use	
C	By taking advantage of signals with a high perceived value reinforcing differentiation concerning essential selection criteria	
	Reduce differentiation costs	
A	Exploit differentiation advantages that cost nothing	
B	Minimise the price of differentiation by controlling the decisive cost generators	
C	Emphasise the types of differentiation for which your enterprise will enjoy a clear cost advantage from differentiation	
D	Reduce costs from activities that are of no value to the buyer	
	Create entirely new rules	
A	Discover selection criteria nobody has yet discovered	
B	Try to change customers' decision centres if that would be to your advantage	
C	Proactive response to buying and channel factors	
	Reconfigure the overall value chain	
	Pitfalls in connection with differentiation	
A	At the end of the day, the unique points will not be appreciated by the customers	

B	The degree of differentiation is too high and is, therefore, not accepted	
C	The extra profit that you are looking for is too high in relation to the perceived added value	
D	The enterprise ignores the necessity of signalling value	
E	The enterprise is unaware of the costs of differentiation	
F	Focusing on the product rather than on the value chain as a whole	
G	Too little attention being paid to the diversity of the segments	
IV	*How can the entry strategy be made to fit into generic product-market strategies:*	

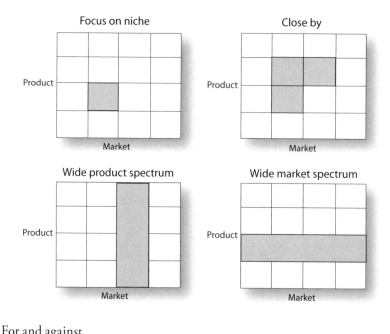

For and against _____

_____

_____

Checklist for entry strategies

The inventory can be used elaborating and discussing entry strategies. It is by no means certain that you can categorise your own planned strategy exactly in relation to the simplified types described in the chapter. On the other hand, the inventory lets you form opinions of a type that is general and, therefore, applicable in very diverse situations.

Until all of a sudden it was broken down, the Berlin Wall was considered an insurmountable barrier. When it had fallen most people wondered how easily and swiftly it had happened and how frail the powers behind it really were.

Literature

Aaker David: *Building strong Brands*. The Free press. 1997.

Aaker David: *Managing Brand* Equity: *Capitalising on the Value of a Brand Name*. The Free Press. 1991.

Aaker David: *Strategic Market Management*. Wiley & Sons. N.Y. 1998.

Abell Derek E. og Hammond J.S.: *Strategic Marketing Planning – Problems and Analytical Approaches*. Prentice Hall. 1979.

Abell Derek E.: *Defining the Business – the Starting Point of Strategic Planning*. Prentice Hall. 1980.

Cravens D.W.: *Strategic Marketing*. Irvin. 1994.

D'Aveni Richard A: *Hypercompetitive Rivalries – Competition in Highly Dynamic Environments*. The Free Press. N.Y. USA. 1995.

Drucker Peter F.: *Innovation and Entrepreneurship – practice and principles*. Butterworth, London. 1986 (1999).

Drucker Peter F.: *The Discipline of Innovation*. Harvard Business Review, Nov-Dec 1998 p. 149 – 156.

Duus Henrik Johannsen: *Economic Foundation for an Entrepreneurial Marketing Concept*. Scandinavian Journal of marketing. 1997.

Hills Gerald et alt: *Marketing and entrepreneurship research – ideas and opportunities*. Quorum books. Greenwood Press Weestport. Connecticut, US. 1994.

Kotler Philip: *Marketing Management*. Prentice Hall. N.J. 1988.

Kotler Philip: *Principles of Marketing*. Prentice Hall N.J. 1980.

Larreché Jean Claude, Gatignon Hubert: *Markstrat 3*. International Thomson Publishing. 1997.

Mansfield Edwin, Schwartz Mark, Wagner Samuel: *Imitation Costs and Patents: An emperical study*. Economist Journal Dec. 1992.

Mc-Kinsey Quarterly 2002. *Just in Time Strategy for a Turbulent World*.

Minzberg Henry, Lampek Joseph: *Reflecting on the Strategy Process.* Sloan Management Review. 1999.

Minzberg Henry: *Minzberg on Management.* Free Press. N.Y. 1998.

Mullins John W. *The Business Road Test.* Prentice Hall. London. 2003.

Parry Mark, Bass Frank: *When to Lead or Follow? It Depends.* Marketing Letters vol. 1, 1989.

Porter Michael E: *Strategy and the Internet.* Harvard Business Review. 2001.

Prahalad C.K og Hamel Gary: *Competing for the Future.* Harvard Business School Press. Boston. 1994.

Prahalad C.K. og Hamel Gary: *The Core Competence of the Corporation.* Harvard Business Review. 1990.

Robinson William T, Fornell Claes: *Sources of Market Pioneer Advantage in Consumer Goods Industries.* Journal of Marketing Research. Aug. 1985.

Sundbo Jon, Fuglsang Lars, Norvig Larsen Jacob: *Innovation med omtanke.* Systime. 2001.

Urban L. Glen, Kalyanaram: *Dynamic Effect of the Order of Entry on Market Share, Trial Penetration and repeat Purchases fro frequently purchased Consumer Goods.* Working Paper. MIT. Cambridge. Mass. US. 1991.

Williamson Oliver: *The Economic Institutions of Capitalism – Firms, Markets, Relational Contracting.* Free Press. 1985.

7. The positive influence of competitors

"We are all good at something.
It's just a matter of finding out what at."

Said by Ole Lund Kirkegaard, Danish author of children's books

The present chapter looks into the following idea: Competition may have a positive influence on the success chances of a new business idea. Consequently, competitors should not be viewed as an obstacle or as threats that you must do everything to avoid. Competitors can be lighthouses, opportunity generators, protectors, pioneers, breakwaters, generous conductors and many other things which, in certain situations will support a small, newcomer enterprise in particular.

Therefore, it is important to choose your competitors carefully – to find munificent environments – seen from the outside. In many cases in which existing competitors in a market already motivate and develop each other, they also indirectly protect themselves by raising the entry barriers – to the detriment of an entrepreneur. Accordingly the argument about the positive effect of competition may be a two-edged sword.

Good business plans always include an unbiased competitor analysis. However, such insight is rarely used diagnostically enough to discover the real minefields and potential oases. The entrepreneur is willing to do his homework, but often forgets to draw creative conclusions from the available information.

By choosing its competitors carefully, the new venture will increase its chances of survival and success considerably.

7.1 Introduction strategy and choice of competitors

The role and importance of competition is dynamic. A newly started enterprise has no experience, but can only put their trust in faith, hope, expectations and a will to make a difference. Synthetic experience should by no means be confused with the confidence and gut-feeling which actual experience gives to a decision maker.

An entrepreneur's situation just prior to market entry is by definition the riskiest and most unpredictable of all in the entire lifespan of an enterprise. And as expected, competitors' reactions are a factor which may be life-giving or the opposite. For this reason it is important to find positive rather than negative environments.

A first mover who has either discovered an entirely new market, or, more frequent, has developed a new, revolutionising product, technology or the like, will see the entry as a race with time to beat potential competitors on the basis of an assumption that the market is ready and that the position as the runner-up will prove to be wholly or partly worthless.

To a pioneer the concept of choice of competitors often does not make sense at all; however, the question is whether, in such circumstances, the concept is correctly defined. If an innovation is intended to replace existing products, methods, technologies, etc., a pioneer will compete head-on with well established suppliers even though old products and structures appear to be hopelessly inferior and therefore no competition at all.

Revolutionising inventions

When the railways were built in Great Britain in the early 19th century, they encountered massive competitive resistance from the canals, a gigantic system of waterways criss-crossing the country, a system which up until then had functioned as an efficient transport technology while being a financially very strong industry. The same applies to Thomas Edison's incandescent lamp a few generations later, which took up the struggle against town gas as a source of street illumination in American cities.

Today it seems absolutely foolish – albeit heroic – that the prevailing technologies did not simply roll over and give up the struggle against such epoch-making and obviously superior innovations like steam engines and incandescent lamps. But in fact they had no choice but to fight. Their market position came under attack and their assets could not profitably be deployed elsewhere. The same is actually true of the challenger – the railway companies of the day and General Electric, Westinghouse and Siemens. For them it was necessary to defeat the existing market logic in head-on confrontation with big, dominant companies. The outcome was a gladiator struggle.

The hypothesis is that in practice most pioneer strategies contain a different and far more direct competition aspect than the race with projects that define

176

themselves identically, and that is the competition with the incumbent suppliers, who may be very diverse, and who are already making a living in meeting the same needs, and whose position is coming under threat.

All other venture scenarios than "first come, first served" have to do with imitation, focusing or differentiation in one form or another, for which reason a careful scrutiny of and choice of competitors may be crucial for survival – a kind of applied Darwinism.

Danish groceries – the COOP as a competitor

"The fascinating thing about retailing is that in a fraction of a second you can measure the effect of your sales endeavours".
Said by Herman Salling, founder of Dansk Supermarked DS about retailing

In the course of a little more than a generation, the legendary Herman Salling and the DS succeeded in developing a highly successful groceries retail group. The DS was founded in 1960 when the first Føtex was opened. Føtex was an entirely new kind of supermarket in Denmark and was based on the notion that customers should be able to buy food, hardware and clothes in one single place. Later came similar enterprises, Bilka, Netto, Tøj & Sko, A-Z, and Bugatti ….

Among many other factors, competition has played an important part in the constant progress enjoyed by the DS. In addition to the independent retailers and the voluntary chains that have constantly had to relinquish market shares, the DS has lived in a kind of marriage of convenience with the cooperative movement, now known as the COOP. In terms of turnover the COOP with the supermarket chains Kvickly, Brugsen, Irma and Fakta has managed to keep its size and nominal lead.

During most of this long period, the COOP has been relatively satisfied with its position and its results in its capacity as mixture of altruistic consumer movement and profit-making business, although major changes in the order of priority has taken place in recent years. To be sure, DS has systematically taken the greater part of market growth, and year on year has performed better financially, has demonstrated innovative ability, etc. – but without the COOP having seriously tried to destroy its competitor.

In 1982, the COOP took over Irma, and 10 years later some Irma supermarkets were converted into Brugsen supermarkets and Fakta discount supermarkets. Over the same period ISO made advances in the greater Copenhagen area and took over large shares of Irma's market and position as the quality orientated food focused chain.

The example is not intended to display the COOP as a weak and passive mastodon who unconditionally surrenders the keys to the market to astute grocers. The constitutional history of the cooperative movement together with its multi-faceted competencies have been extremely strong and have secured the maintenance of a considerable strength despite enormous changes in market conditions over time. Nevertheless, the COOP has been a good principal competitor for the capital chains, because it reacted with moderation and constructiveness and did not attempt to use its – then – far larger resources to prevent others from establishing and growing. And similarly, the DS has been a sensible competitor vis-à-vis the COOP. The DS has constituted an effective protection against far stronger foreign chains with possible plans for conquest (apart from Aldi, and Marks & Spencer and, most recently, Lidl and Rema 1000) and has allowed the COOP to develop chain profiles which in many respects are a match for the DS' own.

You should consider the choice of competitors as a business opportunity when fine tuning your entry strategy. Perhaps the wisest thing is to select markets and points of differentiation in the beginning where one or several competitors provide shelter which will allow the underbrush put down roots and grow. If a new venture gets an opportunity to establish a bridgehead in a market with good competitors – even if not the most attractive – it is clearly preferable to attacking a dominant player, who will do their utmost to throttle an invader.

Scandinavian Tobacco

Following the establishment of the Common Market (the EU) in the late 1950s, three Danish tobacco dynasties – Chr. Augustinus, C.W. Obel and R. Færch – decided to merge. And so was born Scandinavian Tobacco.

After a decade during which the big – primarily American – cigarette brands tried to penetrate the Danish (and Scandinavian) market, one of the world's oldest tobacco groups, British American Tobacco, in 1972, decided to join Scandinavian Tobacco which ever since has been completely dominant with a cigarette market share of over 95%.

Scandinavian Tobacco is pursuing a palisade strategy. By means of its brands and by steering perceived positions towards specific customer segments and their needs, Scandinavian Tobacco has made an effective ring-fence round all consumers. On an on-going basis Scandinavian tobacco constantly checks for cracks in the palisade, for instance, new requirements, selection criteria or segments, or changes to the perceived positions. This is done, for instance, by launching new brands and by means of off-the-shelf projects which they can use if consumer preferences change or if a new competitor appears on the horizon. Scandinavian Tobacco owns the market.

Unlike the COOP, Scandinavian Tobacco will hardly be a good competitor for a hypothetical newly started cigarette producing or selling enterprise with ambitions of acquiring a certain market share. This market will not be worthwhile seeking out if you are looking for a competitor with a positive strategic value, which may contribute towards increasing the competitive advantages for the new venture rather than the reverse. In addition to the palisade such an imagined cigarette venture is likely to encounter a company producing efficiently, having a strong bargaining position in all distribution channels and whose free cash flow is sufficiently large and dedicated to make life miserable for any opportunist.

The room for manoeuvre in the choice of competitors will become narrower once a business concept and especially once a business model have been finally decided. Generally it can be observed that the further back in the chain of supply a company chooses to make its entry among those actually available, the better will be the chances of central competitors following because they will be converted into customers and partners in development.

This rationale has been taken up in previous chapters and is especially relevant in high-tech entrepreneurial situations. Realising the truth of the matter may be difficult, because you have to force yourself into moving your focus away from your original vision of servicing a particular market with a unique offer – an end product – towards a short track to which you are, as it were, inviting your competitors to join you, which means that they will, in fact, profit from the innovations of the venture. This point of view should not be over-interpreted: when at an early stage Lego discovered that plastic was an excellent material for toys compared to wood, which was used in the early days, it would, of course, not have been good advice to tell Mr.Kirk Kristiansen that Lego should become a plastic producer and supply the manufacturers of the leading toy brands of the day with components. On the other hand, at an earlier stage than was in fact the case, Lego should perhaps have accepted that the ability of the company to develop universes and characters(e.g. that of Harry Potter) was not competitive, for which reason alliances with content owners will be attractive for Lego.

7.2 Competitors as strategic midwives

Usually competitors are, quite rightly, perceived as a threat and not as an opportunity. Sometimes, when an innovation is knocking loudly at the door, incumbent suppliers turn on the newcomer instead of aiming their artillery at each other. In a way this reaction can be seen as a tribute to a newly started enterprise, a sign that its entry is being seen as a threat to be taken seriously. Bill Gates, for example, at a very early stage called Linux a far tougher opponent for Microsoft than all the big competitors.

Entrepreneurial experience with international fairs and exhibitions

In a large majority of cases new enterprises are not even noticed or they are shrugged off by the competitors. You see clear evidence of this when visiting international trade fairs. Quite rightly new, innovative enterprises see the big trade fairs as an incredibly important display window. Often an entrepreneurial team will return from the big international trade fairs euphoric with happiness, bursting with expectations and lots of prospects to work on. In that situation you should always ask how the competitors reacted and how much interest they took in the innovation. This question always provokes surprise and confusion. But the thing is that the competitors' reactions during and after trade fairs can be seen as the canary in the mine shaft.

Not long ago, an exciting new initiative saw the light of day – a unique invention – in the form of an ergonomic and motorically well designed computer mouse – which can intuitively move objects in three dimensions on a screen. Patented technology. Skilful engineers on the team. The ambition was to conquer the rather considerable segment for whom 3D-navigation is very important, and who has, so far, had to make do with fairly inferior solutions. It was the hypothesis that imitation on the part of the competitors had to be considered unrealistic. Success was just around the corner.

The mouse was introduced at the leading European IT trade fair, and apparently its reception was enthusiastic. The global computer mouse market is dominated by a few suppliers (less than a handful) with well established brands and strong distribution. Later the entrepreneurs were asked, "What did the big competitors have to say – Microsoft and Logitech who are the best known suppliers – about your innovation (which will undermine their position, of course, if …)?" And, "Have they asked the price for taking you over?" Silence. The big players had not even noticed the venture – protected as they were and are by distribution and therefore by market access as the crucial entry barrier.

The following introduces and discusses a top-10 list of situations in which competitors can act as midwives for a new business venture and create strategic value for it. Situations in which competitors shelter, protect or facilitate. Not necessarily because this is what the competitors intend to do, but because of market conditions and the strategies pursued by the individual competitors. You should see these cases as possible clues for discovering new opportunities and sources of insight into what room for manoeuvre is available in the business context. The list is in no particular order of priority.

1. Competitors create niches for all
2. Competitors pave the way for complementary products
3. Standards/benchmarks as midwives
4. Customers ask for alternatives
5. Competitors throw open chances of differentiation
6. Competitors stimulate the overall market
7. Competitors reduce customers' risk
8. Competitors reinforce success-creating industry factors for entrepreneurs
9. Competitors motivate entrepreneurs
10. A market-leading competitor holds up a cost umbrella

Competitors create niches that they themselves neglect and leave to others

In growth markets suppliers very often concentrate on the biggest and most attractive segments in the competition to become the market leader. Less attractive, clearly delineated segments with differentiated needs – not all fit one size – are not necessarily undiscovered, but are considered to hold insufficient potential to justify the specialisation required to adjust to the niche. So, on the one hand, competitors will stimulate primary demand and, on the other, they do not direct their efforts at less attractive customers, especially not if their needs and requirements deviate substantially from those of the mainstream market.

This may turn out to be the opportunity for a newcomer enterprise. For a long time the big airlines were unaware of the growing demand for low-cost flights in their endeavours to serve full-fare business travellers looking for high levels of service, flexibility and regularity. In the beginning, the entry of the low-cost carriers was viewed with a mixture of scepticism and indifference – although some exceptions did exist – and this, as we all now know, had serious consequences.

The reverse situation also occurs, i.e. competitors are using over-proportionate amounts of resources on marginal customers and thus lose a sense of priority in relation to the most attractive market segments.

Public Service

Railways. National television stations. Airlines. Telecoms. Utilities. Big domestic companies with a public-service obligation as the price to be paid for privileges. Such companies/organisations have lived with an obligation to provide service to unprofitable market segments, and in return they have benefited from protection against competition. Rapid deregulation has paved the way for lots of innovations. For one thing, the old monopolies have been unfocused on growth markets, for another, they have, logically, developed product orientated cultural features and cost intensive routines – factors forming a good basis for new niche-orientated suppliers.

Conquering niches is not reserved for entrepreneurial enterprises alone – but may also be a vital strategic opportunity for established suppliers looking to cultivate their competencies and who have glimpsed a chance of taking a sustainable, defensible position. Nevertheless, it is surprising to observe the ease with which innovative projects can sometimes dig their toes in by laying a firm hand on niches that have directly or indirectly been created by competitors. In particular this happens if the three following conditions obtain:

- Cost, image or system ties make it difficult for incumbent suppliers to adjust to the niche.
- The niche appears to be marginal, uninteresting, inaccessible or difficult to catch sight of on the basis of the existing industry logic.
- Competitors deter each other from multi-focusing and differentiation whereas newcomers will not encounter similar reprisals.

Competitors create a market for complementary products

Hardware and software. Microwave ovens and popcorn. Cameras and films. One-family houses, car sales and lawnmowers. The world is full of examples of complementarity. Many successful business concepts are born on the basis of an analysis of innovations, new product categories, market growth, etc. leading to an identification of complementary markets.

Strictly speaking, complementarity is the opposite of competition. The sales and fleet of DVD-players stimulate the sale of DVDs – not the other way around. The thrust and strength of competition has, however, had a decisive impact on the characteristics of derived, complementary markets – including the question of whether new enterprises, in particular, have special opportunities.

Easybrick

Competition in the market for mobile phones and electronic organisers was very much a question of offering consumers more and new fields of application – polyphonic sound, logos, text messages, camera function, video, data services. The new functionalities require higher processing power and more memory, but also better batteries and more frequent recharging. The market for chargers is complementary to the terminal market.

The innovation pace in the charger market has been lagging behind, as it were, the development of terminals and has so far been seen as a relatively inferior commodity without importance to the consumer in making his or her choice. One consequence has been that the biggest suppliers of chargers, who have shared the market between them, have focused exclusively on unit costs and price, whereas dimensions such as design, weight, electricity consumption during stand-by have largely remained at the same level over several generations of terminals.

The start-up enterprise Easybrick took advantage of this and developed the product platform Tiny Plug, which does not focus on price exclusively but also on an expectation that gradually consumers will be willing to pay a little more for design, compactness, and reduced leakage during stand-by.

Standards as midwives for new ventures

Absence of a standard may block market development. The classic example of this is the competition between VHS and Beta format in the video cassette market. As long as they were stubbornly fighting each other, the content suppliers and the producers of hardware avoided investing in the market because of their expectation that consumers would hold back until one and only one standard had been de facto accepted.

Promising emerging markets and technologies usually attract a lot of entrepreneurial initiative. Whether and when a market will begin to grow will, however, entirely depend on the existence of a consensus for a standard.

In some cases, de facto standards are created as the result of a murderous elimination race in which one supplier will end up as the standard – Microsoft and Windows. The fact that a single operative system now sets the standard has, to be sure, led to the eradication of Microsoft's direct competitors, but does, on the other hand, essentially explain the quick growth of the computer market. The alternative would have been a fragmentation of the software market, far higher prices and slower penetration. In short: poor conditions for slipstream innovation. Virgin markets without standards make the customers hold back.

We see more and more examples of leading suppliers – competitors – agreeing on a common standard rather than launching their own proprietary solutions and starting a war only one of them, if any, can win. As a consequence they avoid fatiguing, resource intensive mutual competition while at the same time ensuring quicker and cheaper stimulation of demand. An advantage will not only accrue to those suppliers who agree about the protocol or the format. Establishment of a standard also means that the way is opened for everybody else who will probably position themselves elsewhere in the value chain. Such a development is very typical in the field of software and telecommunication with known standards such as GSM, Blue Tooth, Web Services, HTML and WAP.

Competitors open the road because customers want alternatives

Imagine a situation where one or more suppliers dominate a certain category of goods and where customers cannot opt out of the category. In such cases it is conceivable that customers will consciously inspire new players to establish themselves in the market, to enter into strategic alliances with them. The customers' motivation for doing so is not exclusively the wish to strengthen their own narrow purchasing and bargaining position but also the objective of being able to exploit the combination of economies of scale and variation. An example will serve to illustrate this.

Private labels in groceries

Growing (price) competition all over the world encourages supermarket chains in general to pay more attention to their supply of goods. In this regard a trend can be observed towards reducing the number of brands in each product category. For instance, from 5-8 to perhaps 2-3. This means that the number of suppliers is reduced by as much as 50%. By concentrating on a few, very big labels the overall profit contribution per space unit in the stores is increased through a combination of higher volume and lower prices.

At the same time, increasingly the chains' strategy will be to build up their own private labels. In some countries mainly in the form of premium products with a higher price than the well known brands. In others, mainly in the form of the confidence inspiring low-price alternative to the dominant brands.

This development means in the first instance that the well known labels get higher exposure in the supermarkets; secondly, they are forced to promote sales more massively, while really paying some of the costs involved in marketing the chains' private labels.

Brand names are in themselves an example of the fact that the competitor – the leading label suppliers – paves the way for alternatives. At the same time, the chains very often need new suppliers from among producers to be able to pursue their own strategy with sufficient bottom-line orientation.

This dilemma represents an opportunity for an entrepreneur to gain access to a market whose entry barriers would otherwise be impossible to scale.

So it may form part of the entrepreneur's manuscript to raise the question: To what extent do the customers of the industry have the intention and strength to nurture new ventures aimed at developing an alternative to incumbent – probably strong – supplier(s)?

The incentive to do so need not only be based on a wish to develop an alternative source or become an integral part of reconstituted ranges. Often the argument will be fluctuations in demand, of which one's present supplier(s) does/do not wish to bear the risk. In short: if a new business venture would assume the risk for absorbing demand fluctuations, competitors will accept that customers stimulate alternatives.

Per Udsen Aircraft Industry and Saab Aviation

Per Udsen Aircraft Industry in Grenaa (PUC) in Denmark was a remarkable and quite fantastic Danish manufacturing story. At a very early stage, PUC saw its chance to get a share of the very considerable compensation orders which arose out of the Danish Air Force's procurement of new fighter planes.

For PUC this was the starting signal of a series of remarkable development and production agreements with military aircraft manufacturers all over the world. Viken, Draken, the F16 programme. In addition, Per Udsen successfully migrated to the civil aviation market with several spectacular contracts with Airbus and others.

At one point in time, immediately before world economy started edging towards a slump around 1989, PUC concluded a noteworthy agreement with the SAAB aircraft division to supply the entire cabin construction to the SAAB civil shuttle-flight programme. PUC invested heavily in building a completely new factory (until then the company had been supplying relatively small components) with the highly specialised autoclaving plant that went with it. Early orders started coming in. The future looked bright.

Not long after, the bottom went out of the shuttle market all over the world.

It became clear that SAAB had seen PUC as a secondary supplier. The primary supplier of aircraft fuselages – a SAAB division – had been running close to capacity and could not or would not adhere to the order prognoses coming in from the sales department because it would mean disjunctive leaps in capacity extensions and substantial investments. Its competitor let PUC into the parlour, as it were. But when the market for shuttle flights collapsed, all orders went to their primary supplier. There was no alternative use for PUC' capital investment and it has remained idle ever after.

Competitors create a basis for differentiation

Enterprises with strong positions and market leadership are by the nature of things frightening as potential competitors for a newly started enterprise, but may also constitute a positive factor because the dominant position – the standard – does at the same time create a basis for differentiation.

The presence of a dominant supplier increases chances of developing a competitive edge for new players who know how to exploit the differentiation chance:

- *Cost exploitation*

Indirectly the market leader pays for the communication costs of the new enterprise: Seven Up was launched as the un-Cola. The Volkswagen as the ugliest car in the world. Avis as the diligent runner-up – the underdog – David versus Goliath. These classic examples of positioning actually have to do with exploiting the perceived position of the market leader, which is tantamount to capitalising on their massive communication efforts over time. What would slow-food be without the massive fast-food movement?

- *Serving up strong sales arguments*

A new product with a favourable cost-benefit ratio compared to the market leader can use comparisons with this company as a forceful argument vis-à-vis customers: market leaders who try to meet customer requirements by means of one single standardised solution will always be vulnerable to new initiatives that are developed to be dedicated to certain segments, or which are better or cheaper on certain parameters attractive to parts of the market. It is hardly coincidental that discount chains locate their stores right next to the leading supermarkets and shopping centres.

- *Channel differentiation*

Choosing alternative distribution channels to those of the market leader or the logic of an industry can, in certain situations, constitute the seed of effective differentiation and be an opportunity-creating factor for new entrepreneurship: mail order sale as an alternative to sales visits, sales through supermarkets rather than through specialised shops, e-commerce, net auctions, selling stockings at underground stations, theatre tickets at the post office and pizzas delivered door-to-door.

Markets with high entry barriers and strong norm-setting competitors look frightening from a distance. On the other hand, this particular market type entails bigger chances of showing initiative if only the gate to innovative differentiation can be forced ajar.

Competitors stimulate the overall market making it more attractive to the entrepreneur

Invariably enterprises with strong image positions will be seen as guarantors of the solidity, development potential, robustness etc. of a market from the moment they seriously commit themselves. They create the market while, at the same time, throwing it open to others.

Any reluctance on the part of customers when it comes to making purchases tends to dissolve when the lighthouse effect becomes apparent. The competitors of the lighthouses decide to go into the market feeling confident of the existence of an opportunity. New ventures that were already under way see the wave rolling in and position themselves to conquer sizable chunks of the new market.

CRM – Customer Relationship Management

In the course of a very few years, the CRM systems industry has grown from virtually nothing to a considerable size with companies like Siebel as the leaders. It is estimated that in 2002 the CRM industry turned over more than $25 billion in software and customer solutions.

The background for this almost explosive development of the CRM market was a mixture of new technical possibilities, far more finely meshed registration of customer data, intensified customer pressure, ever better and more integrated ERP systems, and the new opportunities of the Internet. But certainly also very much the fact that the important international providers of platforms and administrative software with IBM, SAP and Oracle in the lead, gambled on CRM applications for big companies. It created a primary demand for CRM software that these three players in particular introduced their solutions and as such sent a strong signal to the market.

Tom Siebel, himself a breakaway from Oracle, saw the potential of the CRM market from the beginning, and initially it was Siebel who was to reap the benefits of his competitors- stimulation of the market.

Competitors reduce the risk to customers

If your enterprise is the only supplier of certain products, in theory, you do enjoy the benefits accruing to a sole supplier by way of high profits. Conversely, customers have no opportunity to replace one supplier with another. If a product is a component in an overall, integrated solution in the customer's product or is an element of an infrastructure, the situation may easily become problematic and will often lead to a rejection of the innovation in question.

So the enthusiasm of an entrepreneur for being on his own can easily turn into the opposite.

Competitors reinforce successful industry factors for entrepreneurs

Many examples have been seen of how an entrepreneur's chances of success may improve in the wake of investments made by competitors – especially in new markets. IBM's global roll out of Lotus Notes on the Domino server led to the establishment of an entirely new industry consisting of application companies and consulting firms. IBM was in head-on competition with the many start-ups whose basis for existence had been created by IBM and the 120 million Notes-users.

In the years to come, the astronomical investments made by the mobile network operators in broadband licenses are expected to be the feeder for many new competitors who wish to provide services over the new networks.

The telecommunication companies will be faced with the dilemma that either they will have to kick-start the market on their own or encourage competition by giving competitors access to the broadband net.

Competitors motivate entrepreneurs

Undisputedly skilful enterprises, more than anything else, act as motivators and learning tools for entrepreneurs. McDonald's fantastic and obvious competence is a striking example: industrialised working processes, surefooted expectations management, market focus, logistics, quality management, communication and reproducibility. There can be no doubt about the enormous importance of McDonald's for the fast food market – including, of course, its importance to thousands of entrepreneurs. Some of them with the ambition of imitating McDonald's feat success, others with more local objectives. These entrepreneurs compete keenly with McDonald's locally and regionally; they found the path to the market inspired by McDonald's indubitable business success.

A market-leading competitor holds up a cost umbrella

For market leaders to demand higher prices than challengers and followers is quite normal. The high price charged by market leaders may possibly reflect a correspondingly higher cost level that constitutes a cost umbrella.

Markets with high prices always attract new ventures that see an opportunity to make a sure profit. It may make sense for entrepreneurs to find new markets in which the market leader not only skims off the cream in terms of price, but also operates at a correspondingly higher cost level which is, at the same time, a requisite part of what they have to offer.

7.3 Good competitors

Choosing your competitors carefully has to do with pinpointing industries, markets, corridors, special time pockets and constellations in which competition represents an opportunity rather than the reverse. Very diverse indicators may point to especially favourable competitive conditions for new small players such as low competitive pressure, unnecessary fragmentation, high growth rates, imbalance as a result of a sudden shift in paradigm or a technological leap and high cost levels.

In one way it is easier to catch sight of markets or situations in which you only have to understand a single leading competitor and their pattern of behaviour rather than a whole cluster. Whenever "competitive situation" can be replaced by "competitor", your chances of assessing a situation correctly will be somewhat better, all things being equal. Figure 7.1 below shows an overview of four archetypes of market leaders who create particularly favourable conditions for newly started enterprises.

Figure 7.1 Archetypes of useful competitors

The archetypes are particularly good competitors for an innovation and for newcomers; they are simplified and slightly caricatured, however, each one of them represents an underlying, strategic logic towards which it is worthwhile orientating yourself before choosing your arena.

- The Good King:
  - Sees himself as majestic, above the hurly-burly of the street-scuffle, he is invincible
  - Thinks he has supreme latent powers and resources

- Particularly interested in innovations and pioneer if they are harmless and supportive
- Generally wishes to stimulate competition

• The Wounded Giant:
  - High cost, service and price level
  - Losing market shares to followers and challengers. Defends himself by tactical moves
  - Fails to have an effective leadership strategy
  - Forced to his knees. Short-term outlook characterises his thinking. Wants to deflect competitors and followers

• The Cyclops:
  - One-eyed giant dominating his territory seeing every competitor as his mortal enemy
  - Happy with his position. Does not challenge himself
  - Fears cannibalisation. Does not observe early warnings. A bit too naïve
  - Vulnerable to innovations which will offset any existing competitive advantages

• The Confident Tiger:
  - Quick and strong
  - Observant of growth markets and attractive segments
  - Is relaxed about new business ventures; does not consider them a threat
  - Considerable ability to innovate and adjust when things come to a head

We cannot draw the conclusion that it is easier to establish oneself in a concentrated industry with one important supplier or a cluster of relatively similar suppliers rather than in a more fragmented market in which entry barriers are, after all, somewhat lower.

However, new business ventures tend to underestimate the importance of the competitive climate and may accidentally choose the wrong competitors. The notion that competition may improve rather than weaken chances of success, and the notion that the presence of an uncontested market leader may prove to offer advantageous conditions for innovative start-ups should preferably be factored into the business plan of the venture.

7.4 Comparison between useful and harmful competitors

The basis of a new business idea is rarely a careful study of various competitive environments, even though this might occasionally be recommended. Information about one's future competitors is typically only collected and processed relatively late in the process. Consequently the outcome of the analysis is very often a self-fulfilling prophecy, in other words: since this business idea is as excellent as it is, it seems that the competitive situation is manageable. We do not think that anyone will be able to or would want to drive us out of the market until it is much too late to do so.

Accordingly there is an obvious and understandable temptation to view the choice of competitors with complacence: the new venture sees itself as an ant among the giants of the forest and has a completely new approach to things.

Since the identification of useful competitors can be perceived as an opportunity rather than a threat – and vice versa as regards harmful competitors – it is definitely advisable to focus more on this particular aspect when designing and implementing a business opportunity.

Harmful competitors will hit new suppliers hard and efficiently if they interfere with the power balance of the industry of if they appear set to be a threat against profits.

Discount petrol companies

At regular intervals price wars break out between petrol companies. Today the big companies accept the presence of low-price companies and allow them to sell petrol at somewhat lower prices – depending on where they are located. If price differences become too big and obvious, something that leads to shifts in market shares, the big companies will reduce their prices which, in turn, will trigger a downward price spiral until, once more, "good sense" is restored.

This is not how things began. When the global oil companies lost their grip of the oil market following the first oil crisis in the early 1970s to OPEC, price formation for oil and petrol became more efficient, and opportunists saw their chance to set up low-price/low-service petrol stations everywhere.

At the time, the market was dominated by the so-called Seven Sisters; long ago they had concluded that everybody would lose if price competition were to become too aggressive, for which reason, it was not. Any attempts at breaking the unwritten rules by dumping or undercutting were immediately counteracted.

Consequently, the emergence of the discount petrol companies was a thorn in the flesh of the industry; and initially it made a zealous effort to throttle the initiative by preventing them from operating any price differentiation. Later on, when payment cards had become popular, the industry accepted that transparency had come to stay. The oil companies were harmful competitors, but unavoidable for entrepreneurs who saw the obvious opportunities for creating a discount market.

A checklist of what characterises useful and harmful competitors for a new venture might look like the following:

Useful market leaders	Harmful market leaders
• Noble behaviour, follows the rules	• Precedents indicate violent reaction
• Short time horizon concerning liquidity and profits	• No need for short term liquidity
• Flexible asset structure – regulation possible	• High capital investment – spare capacity
• Moderate exit costs	• High exit costs
• Loyal customers with high change-over costs	• Customers' change-over costs low
• Adverse to risks	• Willing to take risks
• Business area unrelated or less important	• Business area of vital importance
• Aware of own weaknesses and costs	• Unaware of own weaknesses/costs
• Well balanced in relation to other suppliers	• Fine-drawn "terror balance" in an oligopoly
• Satisfied with earnings and position	• Dissatisfied with own strategic position

Table 7.1 Useful versus harmful market leaders for an entrepreneur

Source: Inspired by Porter 1981

193

Is it always possible to know in advance how your future competitors will react? The answer almost goes without saying, but it should not prevent you from attempting to form a qualified opinion.

7.5 Inventory: Competitor barometer for a new enterprise

For established enterprises competitor response profiles play an important role expressed through the well-known four elements:

- What drives the competitor – their strategic objectives
- What characterises the competitor's present strategy
- What perceptions of themself and the industry the competitor has
- What core competencies and strengths the competitor can muster and exploit

Even if a new enterprise attracts a great deal of attention in the industry because of its high degree of innovation and the immediate great interest taken by customers in it, it will rarely provoke very direct, violent competitor reactions. Consequently, experience shows that a team of entrepreneurs will be best served by perceiving competition and competitors as positive situational factors – therefore, it is important to choose competitors with great care so that they may contribute to throwing open the gateway to the customers.

Consequently, we may argue that it would be quite a good idea to *seek out constructive competition* rather than attempt to *avoid markets with competition or substitution.* Constructive competition may either be linked to the *general conditions* or to some *specific structural properties,* typically with the market leader.

The competitor barometer attempts to summarise these views as an inventory to help you find the trail to places and times where competitors promote and do not impede if only you interpret the situation with business creativity in mind.

I	*The business idea is superior to those of possible competitors. What generally characterises your business idea in relation to those of your competitors?*
A	There really is no competition against my business idea, so it is a bit farfetched to talk about choosing competitors in our particular case.
B	There is competition, but my product/product programme/technology … is so unique that I do not need to pay that much attention to any competitors.
C	The market is fragmented so it is difficult to deduce any essences or to look for the advantages that individual competitors might possibly add to my new enterprise.
D	All competitors must be considered harmful – so choosing one over the other will not affect our offer.
E	Yes, it is possible that our choice of competitors may lead to addition of substantial value.
II	*Trails that influence our room for manoeuvre and on which our competitors can be seen as constructive in relation to the business idea*
A	There *are* some competitors who create conditions for the establishment of niches that they leave to others.
B	Competitors create a market for complementary products.
C	By defining and setting the standard (necessary for market growth), competitors act as midwives for my business idea.
D	Customers want to have alternatives that they really do not have today. In this way, competitors are paving the way for me.
E	My concept is all about differentiation from the established solutions whose presence and prevalence, therefore, constitute an important basis.
F	Competitors increase the overall market. Pure and simple. And that is a clear advantage for me.
G	Competitors contribute towards lowering the risks as perceived by customers because they will always have an alternative supplier.
H	Competitors contribute towards reinforcing and maintaining essential conditions in the industry.
I	Market leaders are a huge source of inspiration.
J	The leading competitor in the market is holding up a cost umbrella!.

III	**Seen from my point of view, the leading enterprise in the market is a constructive competitor because of the favourable conditions this enterprise creates for new ventures**
A	The Good King
B	The Wounded Giant
C	The Cyclops
D	The Confident Tiger
IV	**I intend to avoid the harmful competitor by paying attention to:**
A	Precedents indicating a violent reaction.
B	Competitors who do not require short-term earnings and cash flow.
C	High capital investment – idle capacity.
D	High exit costs.
E	The customer has low or no change-over costs.
F	The competitor is willing to run risks.
G	The market/business area is of vital importance to the competitor.
H	The enterprise has an unrealistic notion of its own weaknesses and costs.
I	The market is only peaceful because a fine-drawn "terror balance" which may easily crash, is being maintained.
J	The competitor is dissatisfied with his present position

The competitor barometer as an inventory

These and other points for discussion may contribute towards building understanding and preparedness concerning the competitors whom the new venture will encounter once it is off the ground. But that is not really the message. What is important is to choose your competitors carefully so that the presence and nature of competition reinforce the opportunities of the new venture rather than the reverse.

Literature

Guiltinan J og Paul G: Marketing Management: *Strategies and Programmes*. Mc.Graw Hill. 1991.

Harper David A.: *Entrepreneurship and the market process*. Rothledge. London. 1996.

Miles R.E og Snow C.C.: *Organizational Strategy, Structure and Process*. Mc Graw Hill. 1978.

Nairn Alasdair: *Engines moving Markets*. Wiley & Sons. N.Y. 2002.

Porter Michael E.: *Competitive Advantage – Creating and Sustaining Superior Performance*. Free Press. N.Y. 1985.

Porter Michael E.: *Competitive Strategy*. Free Press. N.Y. 1980.

8. Entrepreneurship and business ideas in the embryonic market

"The challenge of assessing future markets for new technologies is to determine the demand for products that don't exist by asking customers who don't yet know about them."

George Day

This final chapter deals with the most difficult situation facing an entrepreneur. And one of the most frequent ones: the product or technology, and therefore the business idea, are new to the world – a radical innovation. So, for obvious reasons the market does not exist. Yet. Will it arise? Can it be created? Although many enterprises, which were later to become successful, were definitely pioneers in their respective markets, most pioneers do not end up as winners.

Being able to assess future markets, including how, when and why an innovation will break through and be diffused is, therefore, one of the crucial competencies of the entrepreneurial process and consequently one of the most interesting themes.

By making conscious use of divergent assessment methods to decode (and influence) the potential market, and by organising the venture so as to keep open the highest possible number of market and technology options for as long as possible, a kind of readiness can be established that may well turn out to be of decisive importance at the end of the day.

The recurrent theme of the chapter is the fact that diffusion of an innovation cannot by any means be seen as an inevitable process, but will always be the outcome of complex interaction between many factors over time. Being an entrepreneur in embryonic markets, calls for a fine-drawn balance between strong visions, alertness and uncompromising readiness to change.

8.1 A different challenge

Whether or not an innovation will break through and if it does, under what circumstances, will, in practice, often be – if not impossible – at least very difficult to predict with any degree of certainty. This situation is all too familiar for entrepreneurs and venture capitalists. So-called killer applications and irresistible technological paradigm shifts do occur, but rarely: to be sure, radial tires did achieve a market share of 50% in 18 months. It took integrated circuits less than 5 years to achieve a market share of 80% in the field of electronic components. Home computers and mobile telephones only needed 5-7 years to achieve 70% penetration; it had taken radio and television 20-25 years to achieve comparable rates of penetration.

At the same time it is worth keeping in mind that, typically, there is an interval of 7-10 years from the invention of a technology or application until production and commercialisation. Since the earliest days of mobile telephones it has, for instance, been technologically possible to commercialise sms-functionality – but it was actually done only a long time into the life of the technology.

In hindsight explanations are usually simple and logical. But in the actual situation you are normally left in mystification and almost unbearable uncertainty about the readiness of the market and the capability of the technology to set a new agenda: when, for instance, will our homes be equipped with wireless communication in all areas from household appliances, lighting, heating to communication of data, sound, images to a domestic intranet coupled to the Internet and PDAs? What is holding up this development? What does it take to open up the market? Will there be a single centralised or several decentralised concepts setting the standard? What is "the next big thing" going to be?[49]

Laser equipment and dental practice

As yet, laser technology has not become the generally accepted substitute for the dentist's drill and conventional dental surgery. Over the last decade, the dental industry has spent vast amounts of money in developing methods and equipment based on laser beams – but without succeeding in getting a real market breakthrough. Laser treatment entails many benefits for patients compared to

---

[49] "In new technology markets, the pioneering technology rarely/never becomes the winning technology, which indicates a high rate of error on the part of first movers". Tushman and Anderson (1997)

conventional methods of treatment, and in countries like the Netherlands and USA, laser equipment has gained some ground, but is still a long way away from having displaced traditional technology.

Erbium and NG Yag are the two main types of laser, and within these two categories there is a large number of sub-technologies. Each sub-technology, laser wave and algorithm has its own advantages and disadvantages compared to others and, subsequently its own natural specific clinical field of application.

The 10 most important equipment producers virtually all have a full range of laser equipment, but based on different technological platforms. Each producer praises their laser wave as unique and generally claims that their equipment can be used advantageously for a broad spectrum of treatments.

Among dental researchers there are two camps when it comes to laser. Critics claim that, so far, no one has proven scientifically that laser treatment is effective and that it is not without side-effects. Advocates of the technology propound the opposite view. Very few dental schools teach laser treatment.

When buying new equipment, dentists lean against science. Some (few) dentists swear by laser and can demonstrate highly convincing clinical and financial results of laser introduction, something that does require considerable capital outlays – at least seen from a dentist's point of view. Dentists who have introduced laser treatment are in a minority of less than 10%, but it is primarily young, enterprising, successful, metropolitan dentists who have adopted the new methods.

Rumour has it that the dissemination of laser technology suffered because early equipment was not good enough and promised far more than it could deliver, which is said to have caused a high rate of incorrect treatment.

It is tempting to draw the conclusion that for the time being the producers of dental equipment have confused or in fact ruined the laser treatment market by competing on basic technology rather than cooperating to agree on a common standard.

It is not only difficult to acquire reliable information about or a distinct feeling for markets without any history – such markets are also treacherous, unpredictable and complex. They are treacherous in the sense that the early customer, segments or fields of application, signalling a sales potential for innovations may drive the new enterprise in a direction which later may turn out to be a blind alley. This, as already mentioned, was the fate of the early PC producers who initially invested heavily in entertainment rather than professional and vocational use.

The issue for a new business venture may be that the innovation – the technology, the product, the platform, the concept, etc. – in itself blocks or constricts the field of vision of a potential future market rather than the opposite. At an early stage, the market perception is frozen as a function of the unique advantages linked to the innovation that are automatically associated with specific customer benefits and thus natural fields of demand or customer segments.

Some of the most obvious differences between well known and virgin business situations/technologies can be summarised in the following table:

Entrepreneurial situation	Known business conditions/ established technologies	Unknown business conditions/ new technologies
Industry	• Risk factors known • Predictable patterns • Known players • Stability and predictability • Critical success factors clear	• Turbulence • Volatility • New unknown competitors • Unpredictability • Competitive conditions unclear
Organisation	• Accepted rules and routines • Well defined organisation boundaries • Conflicts are avoided or moderated • Calculating culture	• Received wisdom mislead • Fluid, dynamic network • Conflicts are encouraged • Intuition
Strategy process	• Convergent thinking • Analytical methods • Focus on competitive advantages	• Divergent thinking • Scenario design • Focus on adjustment and flexibility
Resource allocation	• Known cash flows • Known dilemmas • Clear objectives	• Option based • Iterative processes • Ad hoc assessments
Market assessment	• Structured analysis in known surroundings	• Experiments
Development processes	• Well defined, incremental	• Adaptive, flexible in time

Table 8.1: The different challenge

Source: Inspired by Wharton on emerging technologies, Day et al. (2001).

The purpose of table 8.1 is to illustrate the different challenge encountered in entrepreneurial situations where the market does not exist and there is only a vague outline of possible, future requirements and products. The figure does not intend to say that management under known business conditions is really rather simple, while management under innovative conditions is extremely difficult. On the contrary, the conclusion is to demonstrate,

- That competency requirements under innovation are not similar to the management requirements which an enterprise will encounter later on
- That consequently you cannot uncritically transfer notions of good management practice from big, well run organisations to situations of innovation
- The entrepreneurship in the early phases of a project can be considered and described as a professional competency and, as such a specialised management discipline

Mr Entrepreneur meets Mr Corporate

One of the most difficult, most painful and riskiest passages in the life of a young enterprise is the first instance of management succession, the time when there is a wish to replace Mr Entrepreneur with Mr Corporate – the professional manager and businessman.

The fact is that in the long transition from the unknown to the well known environment, the enterprise needs strong anarchic as well as formalist cultural features, see Figure 8.1. For this reason, both timing and co-existence are of essential importance. Very often Mr Corporate has to leave the project – the enterprise – quickly and head over heels – because it was not yet sufficiently ripe. Then Mr Entrepreneur will enter the stage once again and will try to reinvent the enterprise and dig out its pioneering spirit. Even if you are very careful in adjusting expectations, it becomes clear that Mr Corporate finds it difficult to manoeuvre iteratively, intuitively, and adaptively. It goes against the grain with Mr Corporate's reflexes concerning good management.

Similarly, Mr Entrepreneur finds it difficult to abide by rules and formalities when things are coming to a head. He tries really hard to understand the necessity of them and to observe them, but his mental make-up includes a profound distrust of routines and procedures which, consciously or unconsciously, he will try to circumvent and neutralise, which means that in reality he is sabotaging Mr Corporate.

The different challenge is very much about nurturing the peculiar competency of assessing and stimulating a future, at the moment non-existing, market. Assessing the demand for products that do not exist by asking customers who have not heard about them is a complicated, necessary task for a new business venture. You are listening for the faint tapping sounds, or for something even fainter.

If developments are not linear, but discontinuous, it is important to limit unpredictability and to understand what interactive features may trigger decisive events concerning the opening of a market. The fact that a market is embryonic should never be an excuse for failing to understand the operational factors behind it.

Too many people uncritically rely on the combination of the utilitarian superiority of their innovation supplemented by encouraging expert reports about future markets and positive noises from the early reference customers. These three elements are extremely relevant, but are rarely sufficient, just as they are too inward-looking and reflect a tendency towards selective perception: because our product is superb, a market will be born.

In reality it is important to be prepared to take a u-turn, a zigzag course, to refocus repeatedly if market conditions turn out to develop differently from expectations. The consequence to be drawn from unpredictability is readiness. The greatest risk for the venture is for it to freeze in a dominant logic. Some people call this tunnel vision.

The following tells you how to avoid tunnel vision without losing your entrepreneurial enthusiasm. The pieces of that puzzle are the different approaches by means of which you can act competently, holistically and dynamically as regards potential future markets.

These approaches are collected under the following headings:

A. The adaptation method

B. The experimental method

C. The combination method

8.2 Approach type A: The adaptation method

The question of how to predict the diffusion rate and thrust of an innovation, its product lifecycle and turning points has always been fascinating. For the newly started enterprise presenting a radical innovation this fascination in reality, is a question of success or infant death.

Diffusion of the innovation is not an inevitable biological process, but very much the result of the strategic choices of the players.[50] The Internet diffused very rapidly by means of email and with the browser as the carrier wave. By contrast, e-commerce of the first wave turned out to be a massive failure. All societal sectors immediately and unconditionally embraced emails, whereas nearly all established enterprises avoided staking anything much on e-commerce. Through their strategic rejection, they helped block or delay dissemination of e-commerce until further notice. In a few industries, where logistics and distribution are not of central importance – financial services, for instance – e-commerce did get a fast and convincing breakthrough stimulated by what the suppliers had to offer.

Often imitators profit from the efforts of innovators. A study (D'Aveni 1995) showed, for example, that 60% of all patented, successful products had been plagiarised within four years, and that the development costs of the plagiarisers were only 35% of the innovator's investments.

The strategic decision with the highest impact on the diffusion of innovations is mainly the technological choices and the choice of establishment strategy as shown in table 8.2 below.

---

50 D'Aveni (1995): "Diffusion is especially rapid when: (a) reverse engineering is easy, (b) equipment suppliers help transfer key technologies or other business know how, (c) industry observers, trade associations or collegial professional societies help transfer technologies and other business know how, (d) buyers encourage other manufacturers to become qualified second or third sources, (e) personnel move to rival firms frequently, (f) leaks of secret information are commonplace and not punishable legally".

Technological choices	Choices of entry strategy
Does the venture possess core competencies in keeping with the technological choices made?	Pioneer, challenger or follower?
Does the new technology build up or destroy competencies?	What is the dedication of the venture?
Is the technology compatible and is it based on standardisation?	What are the signals sent out prior to establishment, and how strong are they?
Can the technology be applied by other enterprises?	What is the marketing mix used in connection with establishing the enterprise?

Table 8.2 Diffusion of innovations and some strategic choices[51]

The risk of rejection is imminent if the core competencies of the project cannot measure up to the requirements that follow from the technological choices made. The terribly trite statement ought to be quite superfluous, but in practice it needs to be understood if you are to avoid mistrust and, in the worst case, closure. Often the venture overlooks what is required if customers are to be able and willing to acquire a new technology: documentation, support, the ability to develop, competency to integrate, intellectual property rights and security.

If a new technology challenges or threatens competencies in the value chain instead of the opposite it will, unsurprisingly, be met with hesitation. E-commerce could be perceived as a direct threat to distributors whose competencies and raison d'être came under pressure.

ViroGates

Our chances of treating all the many millions of people afflicted by AIDS in the developing countries, particularly in Africa, are minimal today – mainly because of the price for treatment.

---

51 Choices aimed at developing relative advantages: "Relative advantage depends on the performance inherent in the technology and the intensity of stimulative efforts by competitors offering the new technology. Not even the most promising technology will find a market unless the collective efforts and investments of the competitors to innovate market and reduce the cost of the technology to unlock the market". Georg S. Day et al. (2001).

We know that the interval between somebody being HIV infected and the outbreak of full-blown AIDS is from 5 to 20 years. So, during that interval, the infected person could be compared to a car racing towards a precipice. If you only measure the speed of the car and the distance to the precipice the latest – the optimal – time for braking can be calculated. That is to say, the optimal time for starting treatment seen from a health and economic perspective.

In addition to the prohibitive price for treating the disease, the treatment of AIDS patients in developing countries is hampered by the fact that diagnostics – the speed of the car and the distance – are costly and difficult because the patient and/or a blood sample from him/her must be transported over long distances, and for the blood sample even under refrigeration. To this must be added that everywhere there is a shortage of clinics and laboratories with the requisite equipment.

The newly started enterprise ViroGates has developed a simple, prognostic marker that can be used in situ to analyse HIV-positive persons by means of a urine specimen; in this way the state and prognosis of the patient can be established.

In future, this technology will allow large groups of people to be tested for HIV infection, groups that are not examined today, just as chances of treating them improve in economic terms the better and cheaper the diagnosis can be made.

ViroGates' prognostic kit for diagnosing AIDS improves the competency in the health systems of developing countries as the new method can be used in an extremely decentralised way and can be packaged and distributed efficiently locally and regionally.

The question of technological synchronisation is in many cases of the utmost importance. As a matter of fact, customers often choose the second-best solution seen in isolation if it is indisputably compatible with the rest of the enterprise's technological environment. In many cases companies will react idiosyncratically to offers that give rise to doubts about compatibility, because it would entail costs and friction in cooperation between units within the organisation if technical or information components were no longer in sync.

If an industry standard has been created, or if the innovation can immediately be used by other competing companies, the innovation's chances of acceptance increase. Open source, where IT enterprises publish their source codes – their most precious possession – and encourage developers at competitors and potential customers to test and design in the innovation, can often be an exciting and necessary way of stirring up interest for a new idea.

In Chapter 6 the arguments for and against first moving as an entry strategy was looked at from many angles. The chances of the innovation being disseminated will depend both on supply and demand circumstances, including its thrust and strength and the timing of the entry strategy/ies chosen. And by no means does the pioneering technology come out victorious in all cases.

Growth of the ever smaller computer

Already in 1971 Allan Kay from Xerox, the man whom many people have rightly called the God-farther of the portable PC, predicted that by the 1990s there would be millions of PCs the size of a notebook. It was to be ten years before things really began to happen.

Portability was a vision-driven concept when Adam Osborne launched Osborne 1 which was the size of a medium-sized suitcase with a weight of about 11 kilos. Osborne stressed that Osborne 1 was the only computer that could be stored under the seat in front of you in an airplane.

Osborne 1 had moderate processing power and a frail 5 inch monitor; nevertheless sales went swimmingly at about 10,000 units a month or a total of $70 million in 1982. Osborne was one of the most successful companies in Silicon Valley and was considered a serious competitor of IBM and Apple Macintosh, the companies dominating the market at the time.

Developers at Osborne were already on their way with the next product generation – laptops. Unfortunately Osborne Computers suffered from dysfunction and did not succeed in getting off the starting block in management and organisation terms. Then Allan Osborne himself announced that the new models with far better features were on the threshold, which did not turn out to be the case, after which sales of Osborne 1 ground to a halt. This, on the other hand, led to major stockpiling. In 1983, Osborne had to shut down the factory. However, Osborne's shipwreck left the door ajar for a small enterprise in Texas: Compaq Computer whose first portable product was designed so that it could run all the PC software from IBM. The early version had a weight of 14 kilos and cost $3.950, but Compaq gained a foothold and conquered the global market.

It is of crucial importance to the winning chances of the innovation that *simultaneous adaptation* take place in the channels of distribution – not only at the customers'. And it will rarely suffice for the new venture to gain access to the market through one single distributor or one type of channel – although this in itself may be difficult enough. Only when inter-channel dynamics arise between competing and complementary channels of distribution, a forceful push effect will be generated. This may seem to be quite a utopian requirement: for a small, newcomer enterprise to be able to motivate multiple channels into acquiring the innovation. Therefore, the new venture will be more than happy if only one important channel is willing to carry the product. Market access has been secured. Unfortunately the magic nearly always fails to materialise; it would take far more powerful forces to generate demand for completely different products.

In principle you should also love the early adaptation of the new technology on the part of competitors as they too are working towards the same end: stimulating demand. One of the reasons why over a relatively short period of time, the fax machine came to dominate the market at the expense of telex was that, from the start, a large number of Japanese companies preferred the fax and started a market race which was, at the same time a technological race. Competition stimulates product innovation and channel adaptation.

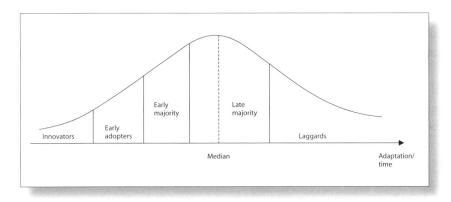

Figure 8.1 The classic curve of the diffusion of innovations[52]

This theoretical model of the diffusion of innovations on consumer markets will be well known to most readers. As a rule, innovators are heavy users, nerds, enthusiasts, individuals with the stature of ambassadors, special socio-economic characteristics, trendsetters and the like.

---

52 The terms technological enthusiasts, visionaries, pragmatists, conservatives and sceptics are largely synonymous with the five innovation segments indicated in Figure 8.3. Huth and Speh (1998). Day et al. (2001).

The adaptation model is very usable for manufacturing markets in which innovators are usually big, advanced companies, best-in-class in their respective markets with high reference values for others both inside and outside of the industry.

The newly started innovative enterprise has to get an informed overview of the conceivable courses of adaptation for the innovation in question to avoid being left in the dark. Who do we think are the innovators? There is no list of correct answers as far as adaptation sequences are concerned. The dogmatic interpretation of the adaptation curve does indirectly prescribe a *trading-down* philosophy: that innovations are first adapted by the top, the most sophisticated customers – the market leaders – and will then trickle downwards from them.

Nevertheless, it is surprising to observe the success that innovative companies have achieved through thinking in terms of *trading-up*: in the early stages they appeal to functionality-orientated customers or segments with considerable budget restrictions. By way of examples, mention can be made of Ecco Shoes, Netto, Nokia and IKEA. Each an innovation in its own field. In the early days orientated towards narrow target groups not characterised by the traditional innovator properties. But, at the same time, they were difficult segments to satisfy and make a profit on. They were all strong so-called best-buy concepts, relying on growing segments. Today they are the offensive, dominant brands. Innovations which, over one generation, have captured virtually every customer segment.

The most critical point in the innovation sequence,[53] some people refer to it as "the chasm", is the changeover from Early Adopters – visionary, analytical, intuitive and curious – and Early Majority – the pragmatic. In this particular phase there is a special risk of the project withering.

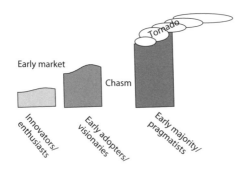

Figure 8.2 The landscape of the technological adaptation sequence
Inspired by Huth and Speh (1998)

---

53 For new technologies, and business-to-business. Compare Huth and Speh (1998) with reference to Moore: Inside the Tornado (1995).

The key to the market in an adaptation context is to be found on the road to the mass market, the road to the pragmatists, the bridge across the chasm.[54]

We know of many divergent explanations of why, when and how innovations are diffused. One main distinction is between *demand pull* and *technology push*.

The demand pull model is based on the assumption of interpersonal communication with an epidemic effect, for example, interaction between users and non-users, between suppliers and non-users. Other models look at the geographic pattern of dissemination in which the spatial dimensions[55] may be *physical proximity* or *hierarchy* in the sense of imitation of the idolised market-leaders.

Some people view diffusion of innovation as dissemination of information; some models view corporate differences as a major source of innovation diffusion and think that innovations are taken on board in step with the renewal of the capital apparatus of companies.[56]

Particularly in the field of IT the analysis of – or the substantiated supposition about – the diffusion of innovations is immensely important for the entire entrepreneurial environment because the value of the ventures are completely dependent on the point of intersection between market and application. Innovative applications are discretionary and often represent a leap. The precondition for demand for the application however, is that the basic technology can take the stress, that the infrastructure is established, that standards have replaced proprietary platforms. To put it simply, the point of intersection between market and application.

---

54 "The fundamental strategy for crossing the chasm and moving from the early market to mainstream market is to provide pragmatists with a 100-percent solution to their problems….. What pragmatists seek is the whole product –the minimum set of products and services necessary to support a compelling reason to buy…..the key to winning a market is to identify a simple beachhead of pragmatist customers in a mainstream market segment and to accelerate the formation of 100 percent of their whole product…." Huth and Speh (1998).

55 "The diffusion of innovation becomes a key variable in the diffusion of new technologies…Uncertainty has a spatial dimension – lowest in metropolises – not just because of infrastructure –but also because of level of information". Huth and Speh (1998). Also Day (2001), Drucker (1998), Tushman and Anderson (1997).

56 8 phases in the adaptation process: "Awareness of a problem or technical opportunity, interest in solving the problem, trial, evaluation, adoption, adaptation, implementation. Huth and Speh (1998)".

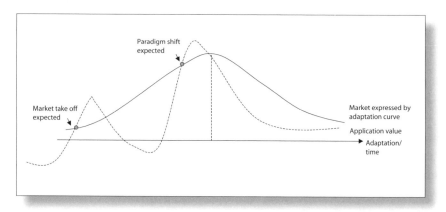

Figure 8.3 Examples of points of intersection between application and market

In the theoretical example, the application has two periods of high market value:

- Prior to the expected start of the market when dominant suppliers try to arm themselves as well as possible to be able to attack the market with complete vertical or horizontal solutions, a time when they are willing to offer a strategic price.
- Prior to an expected paradigm shift if the application is part of the key.

In between – during the lengthy periods of incremental development and relatively predictable conditions – the application represents a limited value, in which the entrepreneurial enterprise will have to concentrate on developing towards the next window of opportunity. It is, however, frequently a problem to obtain financing for these intervals.

In addition to the fine-drawn timing balance in relation to the diffusion of the specifications and price/quality-combination of the innovation, the properties of the innovative product itself to a higher or lower degree, can hamper or foster the chances of the innovation of breaking into the market and being diffused.

- The *perceived benefits* seen from the point of view of potential customers: Even though the specifications and price/quality-combination of the innovation seem to be clearly superior and should lead to immediate acceptance, a number of other inertia creating factors play a role.
- The *perceived risk* seen from the point of view of customers: What if the supplier does not have sufficient resources and cannot maintain and develop

the technology? There are not enough full-scale operations already using the technology. How are our present suppliers going to react, and what are the reprisals they can use? Getting an overview of the consequences in other parts of the enterprise from using a completely new, untried technology …

- Adaptation barriers by way of *fixed investments*: One of the highest barriers that an innovative technology has to surmount takes the form of the investment a customer has already made and that has not been fully amortised. Even though an investment calculation of future cash flows will make it seem probable that it would be rational to phase out existing technological or process solutions, arguments will nearly always fall on deaf ears in such a situation.
- *Reversibility*: The possibility of getting to know the innovation and test its utility without irrevocable commitment. This can be done by means of pilot installations, local experiments, shared development programmes, flexible contractual terms or the like.

Some technologies make it possible to use extrapolation models. Moore's law, which has with great accuracy predicted that the processing power per chip is doubled every 18 months, represents such a business situation. Moore's law has constituted a fairly stable basis for product development among hardware producers across all electronic industries.

The situation is quite different when innovations are abrupt, takes place by leaps and bounds, radical and arguing for a profound break with ingrained habits.

Gision

A brilliant future was predicted for the newly started enterprise Gision. Gision had developed a robust proprietary technological software platform in the so-called GIS (Geographic Information Systems) field. The primary field of application was location based services, hot spots, etc. The possibilities of the technology can best be illustrated by means of a few examples. City buses, for instance, can be equipped with a GIS processor that registers and passes on information about the exact position of a given bus. This makes it possible to determine how well the bus/driver keeps to the timetable. Such measurements can be used in both connection with the preparation and adjustment of timetables and for rewarding drivers for being good at keeping their target schedules.

The city buses carry large-screen monitors. Shops along the route are offered advertising spots at the precise moment when the bus passes the shop.

Gision's architecture was generic and could be used for numerous applications in transport and logistics, for carrying out police duties, in telecommunications and so on.

Gision acquired early pilot customers, but failed to raise enough capital for a real onslaught on the market, probably because the project was ahead of its time, did not have mobile terminals as its primary medium, and did not have a specific field of application in which GIS application would have been a convincing solution to an urgent problem.

Stimuli that increase chances of swifter and wider diffusion of radical innovations can be summarised by the following propulsion model:

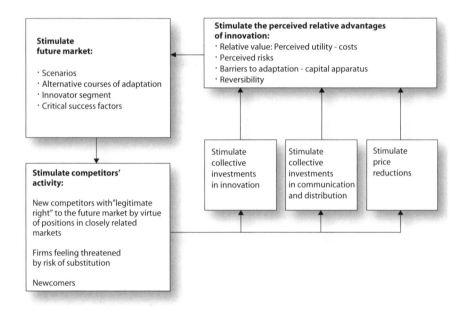

Figure 8.4 Propulsive factors stimulating swift innovation diffusion
Source: Inspired by Day et al. (2001)

The essence of figure 8.4 is that solo performances are hardly likely to increase the probability of success – very much in contrast with the logic that drives many entrepreneurial projects. The positive circular movement in which perceived relative advantages stimulate the market: more customers, higher consumption, more applications, etc, leading to higher demand and increasing

214

interest which lead to an escalation of activities, more and new competitors. These collective investments in product development, higher profile and access will attract customers' attention, increase the number of options open to them and create the impression that the innovation is here to stay.

It should be noted that cost and price reductions compared to the early prototypes in the market will decide whether the market is going to flourish. Shared experience curve for competitors generated by learning, exchange of information, economies of scale, standardisation, and the gradual ripening of the supplier industry play a crucial role, just as competition for market shares and critical mass will force suppliers to sacrifice profitability here and now. Monopolistic prices can be optimal at the very early beginning when the venture is addressing a microscopic segment of technological enthusiasts who must, at any price, be the first to own the newest gadget (consumer goods), but it will, without any doubt whatsoever, be the *penetration price* which gets the market going at the end of the day.

8.3 Approach type B: The experimental method

Palm Pilot

Today it seems obvious that the Palm Pilot was to become the dominant design for a PDA (Personal Digital Assistant) in the early days of this product category. But until the mid-1990s there was considerable uncertainty: many observers thought that the winning design for the PDAs would be delivered by the manufacturers of portable computers. The arguments in favour: portability, user friendliness, and many details. Others thought that a natural further development of the mobile phone would lead to the dominant design of tomorrow's PDA. The arguments in favour: cordlessness, minimalisation, and individualism. Others again were of the opinion that the completely new designs would conquer the market – for example the combination of a pen and a screen with a built-in micro-computer. The background philosophy: transfer of consumer logic from the analogous world, interface, a digital pocket diary.

As we all know it was a radical innovation created by an entrepreneurial organisation which delivered the breakthrough and set the standard. The formula: extremely good understanding of the user, intuitive properties (graffiti!), no shackles to the functional logic of the past.

To which should be added: an extensive use of the experimental method by way of introducing early, incomplete, models with lots of snags and bugs.

They all tried to conquer the PDA market: Apple McIntosh, Microsoft, AT&T, HP, and Sony. Only when Palm discovered that competitors saw a PDA/organiser as a substitute for the paper pocket diary and not as a further development of a mobile phone or a laptop did the real breakthrough come.

Whereas the adaptation method entails certain advantages in theory – the normative logic – the experimental method is based on the principle of trial and error, i.e. *direct market learning*, for example by trying to do something repeatedly, a method also known as empirical logic.

The experimental method means that the market is tested directly for instance by launching early, embryonic versions with the primary objective of learning from customer responses. In this way it is possible to test whether agreement can be created between the technological advantage of the venture and customers' latent or newly arisen needs.

Very few entrepreneurs have more than one stab at launching early versions and have good reasons for wanting to postpone the introduction until the most serious flaws and snags have been fixed. This is an understandable position as capital rationing is almost always an urgent problem. Entrepreneurs prefer to spend their scarce resources on development rather than market experiments that they strongly suspect may turn out negatively.

However, the purpose of experiments is to get valuable information about customers and their needs so that product development can be turned in the relevant direction. Traditional quantitative market analysis, *indirect market learning*, in which customers are introduced to a concept in an abstract of figurative form, after which a number of what-if-questions are put to them, seldom provides reliable answers. In that situation, potential customers are rarely in a position to know how they will react in practice when introduced to the final product.

The best alternatives to direct market learning through experiments are therefore more clinical, desk-research studies of latent needs or trends in which direct feedback from customers is, as it were, avoided. Another autonomous problem with indirect market learning, whether it be done through concept tests, through qualitative interviews, or by means of focus groups, is that it rarely leads to new discoveries, profound ambiguities or strong divergences. Findings are normally largely affirmative, although they may provide correction of important details. This is due to the choreography of analyses, including the maturing effect among participants, who find it difficult to disregard the paradigmatic conditions forming the outline of the analysis. The method is not sufficiently iterative and only has limited predicative value if uncertainty is high.

8.4 Approach type C: The combination method

Potential future customers rarely have the imagination to picture for themselves radically new products based on discontinuous innovation (paradigm shifts) or sufficient insight to relate to early versions of a new technology by means of a notional perception of the final refined technology. Just think what it would be like to form an opinion on the future market for mobile telephones on the basis of the earliest versions.

Although customers' views do not reach far enough into the future they are, of course, the key to understanding problems, frustrations, user situations and the need for changes, and, therefore, they are the primary informants when it comes to understanding the embryonic markets and the dominant selection criteria. But of course, only if the appropriate questions are asked.

The combination method[57] means that the entrepreneur attempts to cover the same central questions concerning the potential future market, but in several different ways in order to lend robustness and elasticity to the case and the decision-making process.

The three following routes can be combined:

- Learning from potential customers who are on the cutting edge of developments
- Learning about latent needs
- Prediction of the inflection point in the product lifecycle

---

57 "It is a truism that prospective customers can't envision radically new products based on discontinuous innovations and judge the early versions of the emerging technology from the standpoint of the refined version of the established technology. However they can be eloquent about their needs, problems, usages and application situations…... But only if the right questions are asked". Day et al. (2001).

Learning from customers who are on the leading edge of developments

Frequently the reason why some customer segments acquire a technological innovation before others is that enterprises within these segments are themselves innovators in their respective industries. One possible way of pinpointing potential customers who are on the cutting edge will therefore be to identify technological avant-gardists in the relevant customer sectors, for example:

- Enterprises in *highly prioritised application markets/target groups* for whom exploitation of the particular technology can help them maintain technological leadership, and who have already worked with or are working with implementing a solution to the problem under their own auspices.

  An enterprise that has developed excellent software for three-dimensional navigation and mathematically accurate manipulation of objects cannot, for example, learn a great deal from designers in web-bureaus, although web-bureaus might benefit from being able to add 3D-functionality to their customers' websites, whether these be trading in furniture, toys, or money. However, the 3D-enterprise can probably learn a great deal from leading CAD/CAM/CIM software companies to whom the 3D functionality is a critical quality parameter.

- Enterprises in *analogous markets* with corresponding applications. The development of veterinary medicines will typically be able to learn from human pharmacology and vice versa.

- Customers who are on the cutting edge because they are involved in *essential attributes of the generic problem*. In the example of the laser equipment Genius – specialised dental equipment for treating and preventing periodontal disease – the project addressed two of the world's leading researchers in the field of this disease and asked them to evaluate Genius through actual experiments on patients.

Since the potential customers are themselves at the cutting edge and have themselves been struggling with the problems from an early stage, they will be able to provide the project with rich, fruitful feedback on the technology in general, application requirements and design concepts just as they will have a more positive attitude to joint ventures and shared development projects in general.

The innovator segment may also be treacherous in the sense that it will focus on a very concrete, possibly narrow, application which may make a perspective relating to wider market segments disappear.

FrontBase

The enterprise FrontBase was established to cover the need for a robust, scalable relations database server. Internet-enabled. No downtime. No administration. Customers used FrontBase to develop everything – from small personal databases to some of the world's biggest enterprise databases (Oracle) – all of them can evade costly database administration.

FrontBase began as early as 1996, and among the customers is a broad sample of segments and applications, among them, the Control Centre for the Copenhagen Police – a 24/7 alarm response system. FrontBase used to have a dedicated support division and special departments for application and tool development, architecture and platform and professional services. FrontBase was the only relation database for Mac OS X with all the properties and standards required of a business application.

In early 2003 it had to close its doors despite the enterprise's unequivocal technological advantage and ability to innovate that had gained broad recognition.

FrontBase might have enjoyed a more glorious fate if, at an early stage, the enterprise had been able to learn from different types of relevant innovators so as to focus their target on specific segments – be they platforms, application fields or generic needs.

Learning about latent needs

Sometimes technological innovation is so much on the cutting edge that not even innovators will be able to provide meaningful answers, or perhaps it seems clear that innovators are not by any means the most attractive customers in the longer perspective. In a situation like that, how do you identify the latent needs of the market? Latent needs can be obvious or less visible. As indicated in Chapter 2, it is a matter of creative market insight, a difficult task when you have to use indirect methods, among them:

- *Problem identification*: What frustrations are plaguing the customers, and what is blocking new technology? When the natural gas project was launched in the early 1980s, it encountered strong resistance among consumers. The problem was that consumers were concerned about the risk of explosions.
- *Storytelling*: Ask the customers how they see the product and what they really think. That is what Kimberley-Clark did; they listened to parents again and

again telling them about diapers. They said that parents primarily do not perceive diapers as a practical disposable product, but as a piece of clothing signalling the development and age of the baby. On that basis they designed diapers that are more reminiscent of pants.

- *Observation*: The advantage of observation is that it takes place in the natural habitat of customers and is not influenced by the scrutiny situation.

Yum-yum OSCAR

OSCAR was an innovation in convenience food, specifically in bouillons, readymade soups and sauces. The innovation was in the packaging and design and quality, and brand nimbus which conceptually differed radically from the market leaders: Nestlé, CPC and Unilever.

By means of systematic, repeated observations of consumer behaviour in supermarkets, OSCAR discovered that consumers make their brand decisions at the moment of purchase, and that brand loyalty does not seem to be significant. The strongest brands (obviously) have the hottest shelf positions in the category, and as a challenger OSCAR was assigned to lukewarm shelves and modest exposure.

OSCAR succeeded in persuading several big supermarket chains to change the relative positions within the category to the advantage of OSCAR, arguing that it would be possible to give a sales stimulus to the entire category by displaying the heavily differentiated brand in a way that would break up a relatively monotonous display of goods. Observation had been the key.

Prediction of inflection points

An inflection point marks a pronounced shift in demand pattern – a Bermuda Triangle – where vessels are beaten off their course and shipwrecked because they have lost their sense of orientation.

Intel's U-turn

Andy Grove – managing director of Intel, the worlds leading producer of microprocessors – has immortalised the concept of inflection point. Grove's message is that enterprises should always be over-sensitive – paranoid – about possible inflection points and be ready to sacrifice any dogmas if the market must suddenly be expected to make a sea change. Until 1983, the Intel business idea was development and production of memory circuits -DRAM. The entire structure of the company, its production apparatus and image was concentrated on memory chips which, until then, had driven the market for electronic core components. Gradually Andy Grove and the management group realised that perhaps the market was changing its character from memories to processors. The process of cognition was long and painful. The overall consequences for Intel were incalculable and meant that departments and factories would have to go and that the heroes of bygone days would have to be phased out. The market had reached an inflection point. Intel's future was dependent on an utterly uncompromising adjustment to the new conditions.

Intel weathered the storm. IBM enjoyed the same good fortune when the mainframe market collapsed.

Figure 8.3 (page 212) depicts the two inflection points, i.e. the starting points and the point of saturation when (when growth rates declines), the very wall that Intel was approaching. Inflection points mean threats to incumbent companies that have their capital apparatus invested in old logic, and they mean opportunities to entrepreneurs who have no ties. Inflection points may lead to paradigm shifts and abrupt change to which it may be difficult to adjust, if there is a wish to maintain strong ties with the past. Please note, that inflection points are always associated with confusing signals and contradictory views – i.e. high uncertainty and unpredictability.

The chances or threats of inflection points fascinate, and there are no simple or single methods for predicting inflection points with any degree of precision.

There will always be many inflection-point prophecies in circulation, prophecies that never materialise. The dotcom bubble is, of course, among the most spectacular of recent times. Expectations of inflection points are created by methodological guesswork, extension of key indicators, projections of lifecycles for products, industries and technologies, gifted case writing, scenario construction, expert reports, etc., etc.

To the entrepreneur, inflection points represent windows of opportunity.

No single universally convincing method exists that will allow us to take a reasonably probable position vis-à-vis embryonic markets. The three analytical approaches: models concerning the diffusion of innovations, learning by experimenting, and the combination method supplement each other rather than the opposite.

The job is not to arrive at a definite conviction about the future, but at an information- based, substantiated expectation of a number of possible futures. Then you can avoid prophecies like the following: "I think there will be a world market for computers of about five," said by Thomas J. Watson, managing director of IBM, 1943.

8.5 Strategies for a new business venture in embryonic markets

Inflection points and the diffusion of innovations are two sides of the same coin. On its way towards the saturation point in one market (memory circuits) the starting point of an entirely new market (processors) is reflected. The embryonic or infant market invites entrepreneurship, because preconditions are undergoing a fundamental change, and because existing companies have built in weaknesses concerning what is new and unknown. This may mean,

- That they latch on to the development much too late. IBM was on the verge of losing its foothold in the market for computers when PCs got their breakthrough.
- That they stick to well known concepts and business formulae. Great grocery groups generally have a weak position in discount chains where the logic is slightly different, and where the cannibalisation risk is obvious, especially because discount stores are located right next to supermarkets.
- That they are reluctant to commit themselves to the radically different conditions. The fundamental change from a world of mainframe servers to a world of desktop effectively killed off formerly strong hardware and software manufacturers who tried to keep up – but half-heartedly so (Nixdorf, Siemens, Olivetti, Prime …). Intel had what it took.
- That this line of thought will restrict their initiatives. Nokia was neither the first nor the biggest in mobile telephones, but achieved impressive results. Nokia is known for its proprietary solutions and has achieved irrefutable success. If in future the decisive selection criterion in the mobile phone market changes from hardware (design, branding, user functionality) to software (contents, services, interoperability), Nokia might get into serious trouble.

In disruptive situations, knowledge – for example about how customers will use technology in the future – will triumph over physical assets and financial muscle. The newcomer enterprise may take advantage of this by learning through disciplined experiments and controlled imagination.

The new business venture with its innovative platform has many chances of developing sound and viable business in changing situations where lifecycle is inverted and new ones make it beyond the launch pad. Below is a list of 10 strategic mnemonic rules- good advice – that can usefully be put on your mental bulletin board when planning the launch of a new enterprise:

1	Keep the organisation supple and network-based for as long as possible
2	Formulate an adaptive and robust strategy
3	Allocate resources incrementally and at milestones
4	Be prepared to adjust technology
5	Focus on the intersection points between markets and applications
6	Understand the heterogeneity of the market
7	Keep a close eye on and in good touch with customers who are at the cutting edge
8	Take good care of information collection about the market
9	Cultivate divergent thinking in your team
10	Experiment

Table 8.3 Gates to the embryonic market[58]

---

58 Inspired by the Kube model – a stochastic project management system designed to ensure speed and efficiency when inter multidisciplinary teams work on the same project. 6 vectors reflect the "wh-questions": who, when, where …. Herlau and Tetzschner.

There is no list of correct answers; dogmatism thrives everywhere. The fine-drawn balance between the force of the vision and the chameleon nature of opportunism is a good recipe for a healthy mix of targeted action and situational management.

8.6 Inventory: Risk analysis and risk management in innovative situations

Good and well-tried business plans for start-up ventures always include a chapter describing the most obvious risks. Uncovering and managing risk must be a core competency in any new business venture, and not a necessary evil that you have to concern yourself with out of consideration for the financial sources. This is especially true in relation to disjointed innovation where the overall risk level is, by definition, extremely high.

Experience shows that risks fall within four categories that can be described independently of each other, but which do interact:

- Market risk
- Technological risk
- Organisational risk
- Financial risk

The previous passages have focused mainly on the market and the question of how receptive this market is to innovative measures. By nature market risk is *external*. In practice it is necessary to look at the overall competency profile of the venture and, thus, also at the *internal* risk factors. The external and the internal risks are intimately linked. An erroneous, firmly cemented, dogmatic opinion of the market may certainly be called an organisational risk, but it impacts on the entry strategy, and therefore on the market risks.

Are strong, unalterable visions and necessary opportunism, the ability to adjust to the market etc., each other's mutual enemies in connection with the start-up of new innovative enterprises? Not necessarily. Take Microsoft as an example. Nobody would want to accuse Microsoft of being deficient when it comes to visionary power. Nevertheless the company kept three projects in play of which only one was to be realised: OS2, UNIX and Windows.

Below you will find a compact, qualitative method to be used to form an initial, overall, holistic impression of the risk profile for a new innovative business venture:

RISK FACTOR		NO: HIGH RISK	MEDIUM	YES: LOW RISK
I	**Market risk**			
A	Informed expectation: I have developed several independent, adjustable market scenarios			
B	Prospective customers at the cutting edge: I have studied and I maintain close, committed dialogue with prospective customers who are at the cutting edge of their own industry			
C	Stimulus: I have substantiated reason to believe that different/several distribution channels will embrace the innovation and stimulate demand as a result of their mutual rivalry			
D	Stimulus: I am fairly confident that several competitors are on the ready and that early competition will enhance knowledge about the innovation just as competition will probably contribute to reducing costs through shared experience curve			
E	I have a clear feeling about why and when inflection points occur			
F	Intersection point: I have a well-founded reason to believe that with this venture, we will hit the point of intersection between market and product			
II	**Technological risks**			
A	It is certain that I shall reach my goal concerning completing the development of the technology and the products I am aiming for			
B	In the embryonic market in which I am going to compete, the dominant design has already been established – or is on the way to being established – and is broadly accepted			

C	All the de-facto and official standards needed for market growth are already in place			
D	As far as can be estimated there are no problems with interoperability and compatibility that I do not know how to solve			
E	The technology is completely producible			
F	My solution is scalable and will find immediate application in a number of contexts			
III	**Organisational risks**			
A	The competency of the organisation has the cores that are crucial for success			
B	The Three Graces – the analytical-diagnostic force, the creative force and the interactive-communicating force, are all strongly represented in my project			
C	The organisation is ready to make a U-turn and to zigzag if the window of opportunity so requires			
D	We have a strong, clear and shared vision			
E	My project has concluded or is on its way to concluding relevant partnerships			
F	There is an excellent match between market needs and the organisation. The project is market driven rather than product or technology driven			
G	The organisation is sufficiently supple and elastic to be able to adjust to change			
H	I am /we are good at divergent thinking. Turning things on their head and discussing them so that the feathers fly. Disagreeing, but constructively			

IV	**Financial risks**			
A	Financing is being made available in instalments in step with arriving at milestones. I am certain these milestones will be reached			
B	I expect that present financing will suffice until the project is cash flow positive			
C	The project does not have to go into a second financing round			
D	The project is financed purely through equity capital and is not backed by loans			
E	The financial structure is appropriate			

Risk analysis

The risk situation varies over time; it changes in step with the maturing of the project and its experimental confrontation with the future market. The overall risk level for a business venture that works with radical ideas, that breaks with mainstream market thinking, or that holds technological innovation will, by definition, be extremely high.

In such situations with many possible outcomes and sudden changes it is important to keep open as many options as at all possible without losing your sense of direction. The concept of *substantiated expectation* means that you will continually attempt to validate and invalidate information and constantly update the risk profile of the project.

Work on *The Business Idea* has now come to an end – for the time being. The eight chapters ought to have made it clear that the book professes to a market-orientated approach rather than a technologically focused or product orientated approach when it comes to the gestation of the business idea. The hypothesis that innovative entrepreneurial ability primarily has to do with understanding the problem so well that you can articulate a solution no one has thought of before is, of course, debatable. In practice talented, customer driven entrepreneurship rarely fails.

Literature

Day George S, Schoenmaker Paul, Gunther Robert E: *Wharton on Emerging Technologies*. Wiley & Sons. N.Y. US. 2001.

Drucker Peter F.: *Innovation and Entrepreneurship – practice and principles*. Butterworth, London. 1986 (1999).

Drucker Peter F.: *The Discipline of Innovation*. Harvard Business Review, Nov-Dec 1998 p. 149 – 156.

Grove Andy: *Only the Paranoid Survive*. HarperCollins. London. 1996.

Herlau Henrik, Tetzschner Helge: *Fra jobtager til jobmager*. Samfundslitteratur. 1999.

Herlau Henrik, Tetzschner Helge: *The Cube Model: a Human Software for training and managing Entrepreneurship*. 1994.

Hunt Shelby D: *A General Theory of Competition*. Sage Publications Inc. Thousand Oaks. Cal. US. 2000.

Huth Michael D. og Speh Thomas W: *Business Marketing Management*. Dryden Press. 1998.

Kotler Philip: *Principles of Marketing*. Prentice-Hall N.J. 1980.

Index

Søren Hougaard

Adjunct Professor in Entrepreneurship at the Copenhagen Business School. Published the textbook *Strategic Relationship Marketing* in 2002 and *Relationship Marketing* in 1998. Founder and Chairman of AMS Group. Former Senior Partner, Deloitte Management Consulting and Chief Executive Officer, AIM Management A/S. Board member in a number of companies and co-owner of several enterprises in IT, electronics, telecommunications and professional services. Strategy advisor for top management in large national and international corporations. Søren Hougaard holds a MsC from the Århus Business School and an MBA from INSEAD.